Inspiring Tranquility

Stress Management and Learning Styles in the Inclusive Classroom

JANET O. GALLAHER AND REBECCA O. NUNN

IUPU COLUMBUS
LIBRARY

The Inspired Classroom Series

NEA PROFESSIONAL LIBRARY

ADVISORY PANEL

Bonnie Bergstrom
Reading Resource Teacher
Westridge Elementary School
West Des Moines, Iowa

Dr. Valerie Cowart
Music Director
New Searles Elementary School
Nashua, New Hampshire

Michael D. Foster
Classroom Teacher
Summerfield Elementary School
Seneca, Kansas

Dena Guttman
Author and Retired Educator
Passaic, New Jersey

Carolyn Pembroke Jones
Elementary School
Guidance Counselor
Tallahassee, Florida

Debra Oehlberg
Learning-Disabled Teacher
Aiken County Public Schools
Aiken, South Carolina

Dr. John G. Porter, Ph.D., M. Ed.
Special Education Teacher
Middletown Schools
Middletown, Ohio

I. B. Van de Workeen
Retired Chemistry Teacher
Retired Pharmacist
Lakehurst, New Jersey

Copyright © 1998 National Education Association of the United States

Printing History
    First Printing: May 1998

Note: The opinions expressed in this publication should not be construed as representing the policy or position of the National Education Association. Materials published by the NEA Professional Library are intended to be discussion documents for educators who are concerned with specialized interests of the profession.

This book is printed on acid-free paper.   This book is printed with soy ink.

Library of Congress Cataloging-in-Publication Data

Gallaher, Janet O.
    Inspiring tranquility: stress management and learning styles in the inclusive classroom / Janet O. Gallaher, Rebecca O. Nunn.
        p.   cm. — (The inspired classroom series)
    Includes bibliographical references (p.).
    ISBN 0-8106-2952-6 (pbk.)
    1. Teachers—United States—Job stress. 2. Stress management—United States. 3. Stress management for children—United States. 4. Inclusive education—United states. I. Nunn, Rebecca O. II. Title. III. Series.
LB2840.2.G35   1997   97-35831
371.1'001'9—dc21      CIP

Contents

PREFACE 7

ACKNOWLEDGEMENTS 9

PART I: FOCUS ON THE TEACHER

Chapter 1. Fight, Flight & Fright Response 15
    What Triggers the F/F/F Response? 16
    The Impact of the F/F/F Response..17
    Interrupting the F/F/F Response in the Classroom 18

Chapter 2. Relaxation 21
    Breaking the Anxiety Cycle..22
    Breathing Deeply 23
    Stretching Tight Muscles 25
    Rory's Story...30

Chapter 3. Taking Care of Your Own Stress 33
    Teacher, Heal Thyself 33
    Sometimes Students Know Best 34

Chapter 4. Taking Control..39
    Establishing a Sense of Control..40
    Working with Children 40

Chapter 5. Shifting Gears/Alertness 47
    Using Sensory Input...47
    Changing How Alert You Feel 48
    Sensory Motor Preference 50
    Slowing Down 54

Chapter 6. Self-Observation...57
    Vincent's Story 57
    Ms. Benton's Story 58
    Jake's Story 59
    Mitch's Story...61

PART II: FOCUS ON THE STUDENT

Chapter 7. Learning Styles 65
- Identifying Learning Styles 66
- Using Learning Styles To Reduce Stress 75
- Matching Learning Styles and Teaching Styles 77

Chapter 8. At-Risk Students 79
- Learning Stress Management 80
- Using Self-Understanding To Make Good Choices 82

Chapter 9. Attention Deficit/Hyperactive Disorder Student .. 85
- Sources of Stress 85
- Taking Control 88

Chapter 10. Hidden Disorders 91
- Low Muscle Tone 92
- Sensory Motor Deficits 94
- Sensory Defensiveness 97
- Optimum Levels of Arousal 98
- Providing Accommodations 101

Chapter 11. Re-framing Mind-Set 105
- Creating an Atmosphere for Learning 106
- Re-framing the AD/HD Student 111

BIBLIOGRAPHY 113

This book is dedicated to our families. It's so wonderful to like them, as well as love them!
To Mim and Papa
To my husband, Jim, our children, Jamie and Katie, and our daughter-to-be, Amy

—Janet

To my children, Susan McCurren and David Pearl
To Susan's husband, Terry McCurren, my other son, and to my grandchildren
To Griffin and Janie McCurren, kindred spirits, and
To Bill McCabe and friends, my West Virginia family

—Becky

Preface

I handed a book to a teacher friend one morning and smiled expectantly as she read the title, which had to do with reducing stress. Before I could say, "I think this is a good book," she looked at me as if I were crazy.

"I don't have time to read anything about dealing with stress! I'm just trying to survive!"

I knew she was having "that kind of year." That's why I'd given her the book. But I also understood what she meant when she said she didn't have time to read about stress. She was literally having too much stress to read a book about how to deal with it.

If you have felt this way before, or known anyone who has been in this situation, then you have picked up the right book. And here's why. Number one: It's not long. Number two: It's written by two people who have "been there" and refuse to go back—a physical therapist working in a school setting, and a teacher. And number three: This teacher called this physical therapist two years ago and said, "If I don't handle this fourth period class better, I don't see how I'm going to make it through the year. Please, bring all those stress things you've been giving talks about and help me!"

Janet came the next afternoon. She taught students and teacher together the importance of relaxation and learning. But most important, she helped me learn to relax "at will" at different times throughout the day—and especially right before this particular group of students "hit" my room.

In the days that followed, the students and I did our deep breathing together and we laughed more. We used our stress balls. We kept the fluorescent lights off whenever possible. If someone came into the room and flipped on the light when we were working, the groans and cries of outrage quickly made that person flip the light back off. I noticed if I began to breathe shallow because David had jumped out of his chair fourteen times in ten minutes. One of the students would say, "Mrs. Nunn...deep breath," and another would say, "David, here, use my theraputty a little while."

We were recognizing the signs of stress and taking care of it together. Other teachers who had some of these students began asking questions and getting answers. Teachers from other schools were saying to their principals, "Get that physical therapist over here to talk to us."

Inspiring Tranquility is the result of our work together. Even though this book is a collaborative effort, we've written as one voice. There are times, however, when we've found it helpful to make the distinction between my experience as a teacher and Janet's experience as a physical therapist.

This is what Janet and I hope to do with this book:

- discuss the overwhelming impact that stress has on our ability to teach and our ability to learn;

- describe how learning styles and stress reducers fit into the picture; and

- explain why the student who is doing everything but turning his or her desk upside down and chewing on it may not be doing this to "yank your chain."

It is our hope that taking the time to read this book will help you—and help you help your students—reduce stress and be more productive teachers and learners.

Acknowledgments

"It takes a village to raise a child" is not a new concept, but it has taken on a new dimension for me. It takes all of us—parents, teachers, counselors, principals, physical therapists, occupational therapists, nurses, clinical psychologists and physicians—to understand what a child needs in order to learn.

The connection between the mind and body, mental and physical, has just begun to be understood. Five years ago, I noticed that the simple act of taking three big breaths and relaxing seemed to have a profound effect on children called "behavior disordered." My search to understand "why?" has been the beginning of a fascinating adventure. Along the way, wonderful people have taught me what teachers and children really need in order to teach and learn. Without the benefit of their knowledge and encouragement, there would not be a book.

The heartfelt thanks of both authors go to:

Joan Borysenko, Ph.D., for lending generous portions of her book, *Minding the Body, Mending the Mind*. Thank you for changing our lives with your mind/body research.

Sherry Shellenberger and Mary Sue Williams, occupational therapists and authors of *How Does Your Engine Run?*. Thank you for giving us a way to use Sensory Integration principles in the public schools.

Pat Wilbarger, M.Ed., OTR, FAOTA, and Julia Wilbarger, MS, OTR, for their enlightening workshop: "Sensory Defensiveness and Related Social/Emotional and Neurological Problems," and for allowing us to use excerpts from their book: *Sensory Defensiveness In Children Aged 2–12*.

Drs. Rita Dunn and Ken Dunn for the use of their invaluable work, especially the "Learning Styles Inventory."

Dr. Agnes Risko, clinical psychologist and physical therapist, for sending positive feedback from Budapest, Hungary. Please accept my gratitude for teaching me that the most important tool the therapist can use toward teaching relaxation techniques is her own inner tranquility.

Patti Benton, teacher of "behavior disordered" children, saviour *summa cum laude* and dear friend.

Jeanne Nunn Lafser, illustrator, friend and believer.

Friends and workmates in the Jefferson City Public Schools and the Special Learning Center: Debbie Hatcher, Mary Owens, Terry Lyskowski, Pam Steenbergen, Marlene Chapman, Mary Wright, Jeanne Sill, Schelly Smith, Carol Roark, Virginia Thompson, Ann Lane, Jeanne Johnston, Janie Johnson, Linda Tetley, Marcia Heberle, Sandi Groetsch, Sharon Gonder, Rita Reed, Anita Glascock, Patty Morrow, Alvin Toebben, Dr. John Sennott, Dr. Bob Steffes, Dr. Arthur Allen, Debbie Hamler, Cheryl Baker, Terri McNevin, Cathy Hubbard, Mary Beth Hoey, Donna Downing and Tami Kirchner.

Dr. Gene Rooney, pastor, teacher, lecturer, psychotherapist, and author.

Jim Gallaher, Editor-in-Chief.

Bill McCabe, who received equal amounts of "praise and cussin" from us for saying, "You can do it. So do it!," first with seminars, then with this book. His belief in us never faltered, even when ours did.

Timothy Crawford, our publisher, who got as excited about our "message" as we did, and who said: "Let's do it!"

And to our dear students, especially Curtis, Matt, Sam, Fred, Jim, Mitchell, Billy, Cory, Brett, Victor, Jennifer, Catherine, DeMarco, Jesse, Chris, Melvin, Andrew, and Larry—our partners in learning.

PART I

Focus on the Teacher

If you fail to make time for yourself, always putting other things first, you will never be happy, nor will you make others happy.

—Joan Borysenko, Ph.D.

CHAPTER 1

Fight, Flight & Fright Response

Stress has an overwhelming impact on our ability to teach and our ability to learn. The easiest way to recognize the presence of stress in our lives is to look at our bodies. The physical signs and symptoms are very subtle and easy to overlook. But when you know what to look for, they are very easy to recognize.

One of the most easily identified symptoms of stress is muscular tension. On my desk I have a picture of a poor little cat who has looked forward to a day of relaxing in the sunshine. But he is so stressed that his body has become as stiff as a board and he can't relax at all. Have you ever felt this way when you lie down for a much needed nap or go to bed at night? The cat is experiencing just one of the symptoms of the stress response and doesn't know what to do about it.

> **Stress response:** Automatic physiologic response of the body (fast, shallow breathing; increased muscular tension; increased blood flow to muscles; increased heart rate; increased blood pressure; adrenalin production, etc.) when experiencing a threat or perceived threat.

WHAT TRIGGERS THE F/F/F RESPONSE?

The fight, flight and fright response (f/f/f) is our bodies' reaction to stress. It takes place when we are experiencing a threat or a perceived threat. This response once served us well: when primitive people were struggling for survival on a daily basis, the f/f/f response put their senses on alert. Their bodies immediately "revved up" when they heard the cracking of a twig in the forest, saw a slight movement out of the corner of their eyes, smelled a noxious odor, or felt something strange brush against them in the dark. All human senses have a direct connection to the arousal center of the brain and can prepare the body to protect itself at a moment's notice. This is why our external environment has such a powerful influence (via our senses) on our internal environment.

However, as a recent article in Time points out, the f/f/f response has really outlived its usefulness. When our earliest ancestors lived in hunter-gatherer societies, the f/f/f response kept them alive. As society became mainly agricultural, the f/f/f response became less necessary for our survival. Although society changed, our bodies

Fig 1–1. The fight, flight, and fright response.

didn't. The f/f/f response continued to release powerful (and potentially harmful) chemicals into our bodies in reaction to the stressors of everyday life. Fortunately, people were able to "work these chemicals out" of their systems because agrarian living called for so much heavy physical labor. As society became more and more industrialized, however, less physical and more mental activity became the norm.

In today"s society, information overload, a frenetic work and social pace, rapid technological changes, and complex family dynamics contribute to our stress load. Our bodies still continue to release f/f/f hormones, but heavy physical labor is no longer a part of our daily routines. So we "sit on our chemicals," and our bodies are unable to metabolize them. Instead they are allowed to "float" in our systems—and that's not good!

THE IMPACT OF THE F/F/F RESPONSE

In the last twenty years, research has produced information that helps us understand the physical impact of the f/f/f response. Dr. Joan Borysenko, author of *Minding the Body, Mending the Mind*, says that even small stressors—such as hearing "Boo!"—will cause enough adrenaline to be released to cause an immediate decline in lymphocytes that augment the immune system. Other physical changes take place as well, including fast, shallow breathing; increased muscular tension; increased blood flow to muscles; increased heart rate; increased blood pressure; and increased adrenaline production. When we have no way of releasing this heightened energy, we may get headaches, high blood pressure, or an ulcer.

In the 1940s, research on the hypothalamus of a cat brain revealed that electrical stimulation could produce two diametrically opposed energy states: One state was a kind of "passing gear" (later to be named the fight/flight/fright response) that prepared the body for survival. The other state (later to be named the relaxation response) was a kind of very low energy expenditure characterized by deep rest and relaxation—the body equivalent of "neutral." When we don't need the extra energy it takes to "pass," we are better off in neutral.

But how do we get there?

INTERRUPTING THE F/F/F RESPONSE IN THE CLASSROOM

One key to interrupting the f/f/f response is to figure out how best to release our energy bursts. It helps to understand how much of the brain's surface area is used for the mouth and hands. These are the two most sensitive parts of the body. When we allow students to hold something in their hands that is pleasing to them (stress balls, balloons with flour, theraputty) and allow them to put something in their mouths (to eat, drink, or suck on), we are helping them create a calm internal environment.

We can also make modifications in the external environment that inspire relaxation. Small changes in the classroom—such as incandescent lamp lighting, fragrance, a cozy corner for reading or relaxation, a glass jar with hard candy on the teacher's desk, stress balls and other manipulatives—can help students calm down, setting the stage for learning.

You might say: "I have a schedule to keep. The students will just have to settle down when it's time to sit in their seats. I can't spare the five minutes it takes to have them take three big breaths to relax or play with things." However spending "five minutes to relax" can be a wise investment of time and a savings in emotional cost. First, research now says that if a child becomes too stressed, the neurotransmitters in the brain actually cause the synapses to close. In other words, if that child doesn't relax, he or she won't be able to learn a thing! And second, if only two students are having trouble settling down, they can disrupt the harmony of the whole class. So taking five minutes to calm those two benefits the whole group. You will also be amazed at how the entire class looks forward to their relaxation time.

Andy's Story

I use relaxation time in all my classes, but one particular resource class really looked forward to coming in at the end of the day and doing their deep breathing and relaxing with the lights out. One student, Andy, especially looked forward to this time. He told me once that he felt like a runaway train by the end of the day.

Andy was "revved" most of the time (he could do his homework best while kicking a soccer ball against his wall while studying), but he was a considerate, personable young man, and I'd never seen him become "physical." One afternoon right after the students had come in and started relaxing, another student from the class next door walked in unannounced, flipped on the light and laughed loudly.

My mouth didn't even make it open to reprimand our unwanted intruder. Andy leaped out of his seat, grabbed the student by his shirt and the seat of his pants and sent him rather swiftly through our swinging door, back into his own class.

Then he calmly turned the lights back off and went back to his seat to relax. I was so surprised, I didn't say a word about his rather rough handling of the boy. Besides, I had an inkling that if Andy had had that kind of day and needed this relaxation time so badly, he might send me exiting through the swinging door if I spoiled "relaxation" a second time!

Learning to Calm Down

There are several times during the day when you are likely to see students in a "revved-up" state. It's fairly common when they are coming off the bus in the morning, or coming back to class after recess or P.E. Any time students are physically active, there's a good chance that the flight part of the f/f/f response will become stimulated sending the child "out of control." Most children are able to make the transition from the bus or playground well enough, but a child with sensory defensiveness or

AD/HD is going to have difficulty telling his autonomic nervous system "Everything's okay. It's time to stop fleeing now." Until teachers are able to help students "shift gears" and get calm, we will not be able to teach children anything.

Just understanding the power of the f/f/f response on the human physiology is a great stress reducer for teachers, who will begin to understand that behaviors that appeared to be directed at them just to make their lives miserable are mostly reflexive actions of the f/f/f response. These behaviors are simply the results of an immature or unbalanced nervous system that has not learned how to adjust its actions in response to its environment. We, as teachers, need to know that we shouldn't even try to teach a child who is under the influence of the f/f/f response. This is an impossible situation for both the teacher and the student.

In order to shift from a state of anxiety to a state of relaxation, students need to know how it feels to be relaxed. A student saying "Teacher, I am so over-stimulated now, I can't think. Can I take five minutes to get myself calmed down?" will save an enormous amount of energy for the teacher and the class. The child could then sit on the floor, back supported against the wall, listen to a relaxation tape, and come back to the group when he or she is capable of learning. If children can recognize when they feel anxious and what they need to calm down, they have a skill they can use for a lifetime.

CHAPTER 2

Relaxation

Relaxation:

> "The body's innate ability to lower blood pressure and reduce heart rate; slow breathing rate; stabilize blood flow to muscles; increase blood flow to brain."
> —Minding the Body, Mending the Mind

> "Produces a feeling of warmth and rested mental alertness."
> —The Brain

> "May be induced by deep breathing, stretching tight muscles/exercise or meditation."
> —Owner's Manual for the Brain

Dr. Joan Borysenko has been teaching her patients the value of being able to elicit the "relaxation response" at her Mind/Body Clinic for over 20 years. In her book, *Minding the Body, Mending the Mind* (1987), Borysenko writes: "Many of us are used to being at the beck and call of the world....You must make time for yourself. If you fail to make time for yourself, always putting other things first, you will never be happy, nor will you make others happy."

This statement really touched a nerve when I read it. At first, I thought it was an overstatement. But the more I thought about it, the more I realized it is exactly right. I think every person in a service profession has a predisposition to give too much of him- or herself away. I would say that physical therapists and teachers certainly have that potential!

BREAKING THE ANXIETY CYCLE

Have you heard of the "teapot theory?" It goes like this: People are like teapots. For every good thing you do for others, you pour a little bit of yourself out. This is all well and good. But when the teapot becomes empty and has nothing else to pour out, it is time to pour something back in again.

Teachers are like teapots. They empty themselves out every day. Unless they learn how to put something back each day, the value of what they have to give becomes less and less. After so many years of being an empty teapot, a wonderful teacher becomes only a mediocre teacher. Borysenko teaches us how to put something back into the teapot by inducing the "relaxation response."

To induce this desired response, we must first learn how to break the anxiety cycle. An example of the anxiety cycle occurs when we say to ourselves: "These kids just have to learn this material before the state's mastery tests begin!" We begin to feel threatened by a job that seems insurmountable. According to Borysenko, our thought process becomes unbalanced and begins "awfulizing" or "one track thinking." Our autonomic nervous system takes over and produces the physical symptoms of the f/f/f response.

Fig 2–1. The Anxiety Cycle

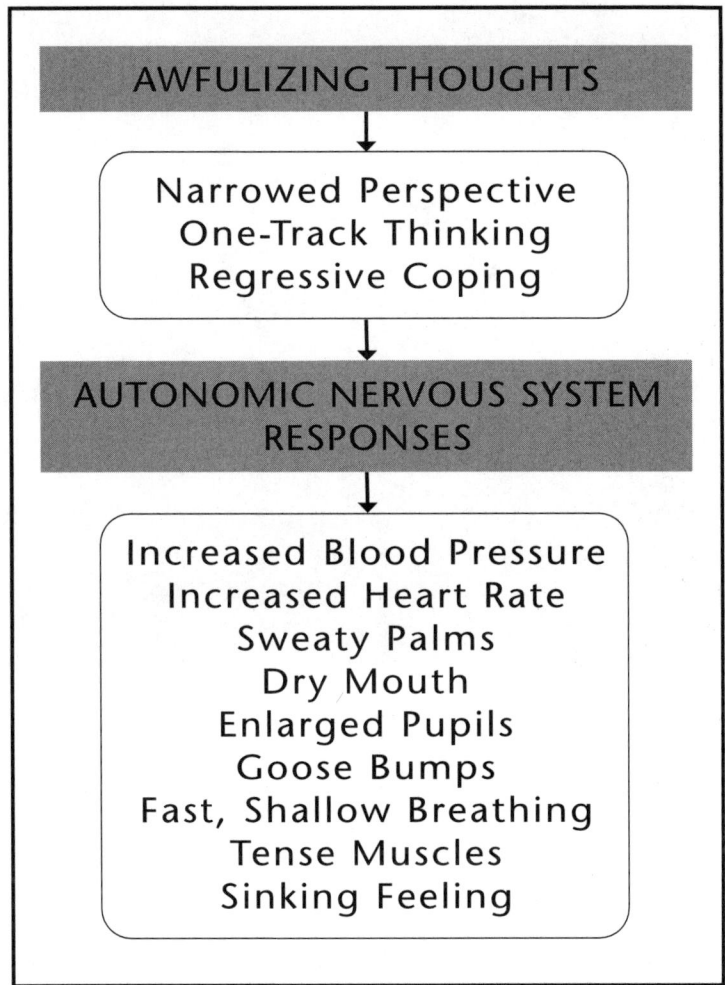

BREATHING DEEPLY

We can stop the f/f/f cycle, and begin the relaxation response, through deep breathing and muscle stretching. Deep breathing calms us down and interrupts the f/f/f cycle. Take three deep breaths at peak stress times for your classroom—for example, first thing in the morning, after recess or P.E., after lunch, and before dismissal. Other times might include fire drills, field trips, or major test days.

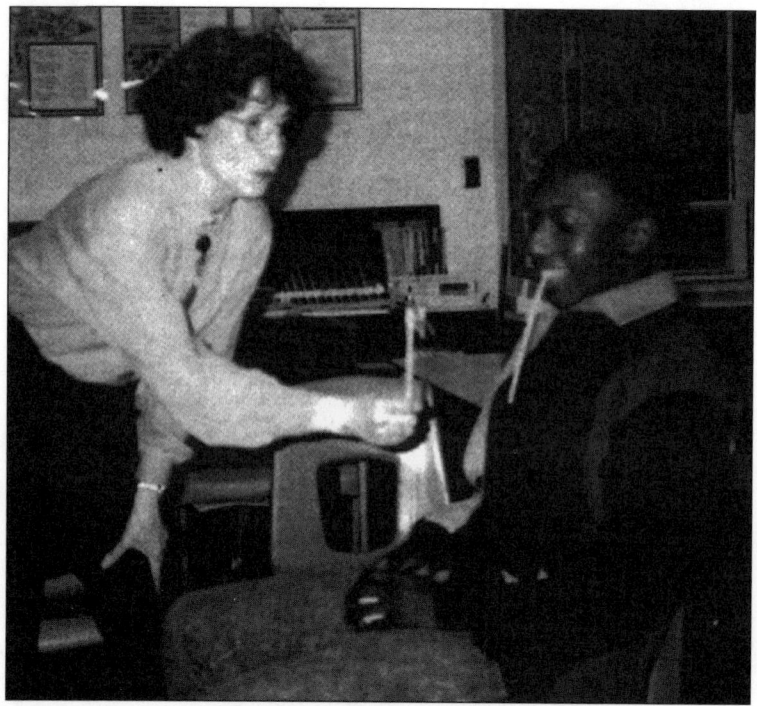

Fig. 2–1. Straws and a small windmill are simple tools used to help teach deep breathing to students of all ages.

You may discover that some children have difficulty breathing in through their noses and out through their mouths. You can teach deep breathing by using a straw to help these children isolate nose and mouth functions. Have the children put straws in their mouths. They should keep their mouths closed and breathe in through their noses, trying to fill up their lungs as much as possible. Tell them to exaggerate when breathing in by puffing their tummies and chests outward and shoulders upward to allow for lung expansion. They should hold a big breath for four seconds before blowing out slowly through the straw. Have them hold their index fingers out in front of their straws to feel the stream of air created by blowing out. It is the gradual, slow release of the air that helps us relax. Tell them to do this two more times and be aware of the relaxed sensation they feel afterward.

Most children with good body awareness will be able to breathe in through their noses and out through their mouths without difficulty. Still, each child should make a little circle with the mouth and blow out onto a raised index finger. "Feeling" the force of air on the finger helps the children slow their breathing. Small windmills can also help illustrate what a slow, steady stream of air looks like.

You can make a game of this: children who are able to "blow out" for the longest period of time are the winners of the "breathing game." In one of my ninth grade English classes, Matt looked forward to beginning relaxation exercises every day. While we were doing the deep breathing, I thought he was faking how long he could blow out, so I went on with class, ignoring what I thought was an attention-getting device. Suddenly, he looked straight at me, hurt all over his face, and said, "I won and you didn't even notice!" I watched him more closely after that, and complimented him profusely on his breathing feat (because with this particular student it was about all I could praise!) Other students even checked to see if he was indeed "cheating." He wasn't. So aside from giving me something to commend him for, it also slowed him down considerably, helped keep him out of trouble, and gave me more time to teach.

STRETCHING TIGHT MUSCLES

The second way to produce the relaxation response in the classroom is by stretching tight muscles. Establishing a daily routine that includes taking three big breaths and stretching is an excellent mood setter for your classroom. (It's also a wonderful life skill to teach your students!)

The following four exercises can easily be done in the classroom. All exercises should be done slowly and stopped immediately if pain occurs.

The Back Relaxer

Our back extensor muscles get stiff quickly because they have an enormous job holding our bodies erect against gravity. Also the proximity of many nerve roots entering and leaving the spinal cord through the spinal column to the back extensor muscles heightens the probability of back discomfort or pain.

Fig. 2–2. The Back Relaxer

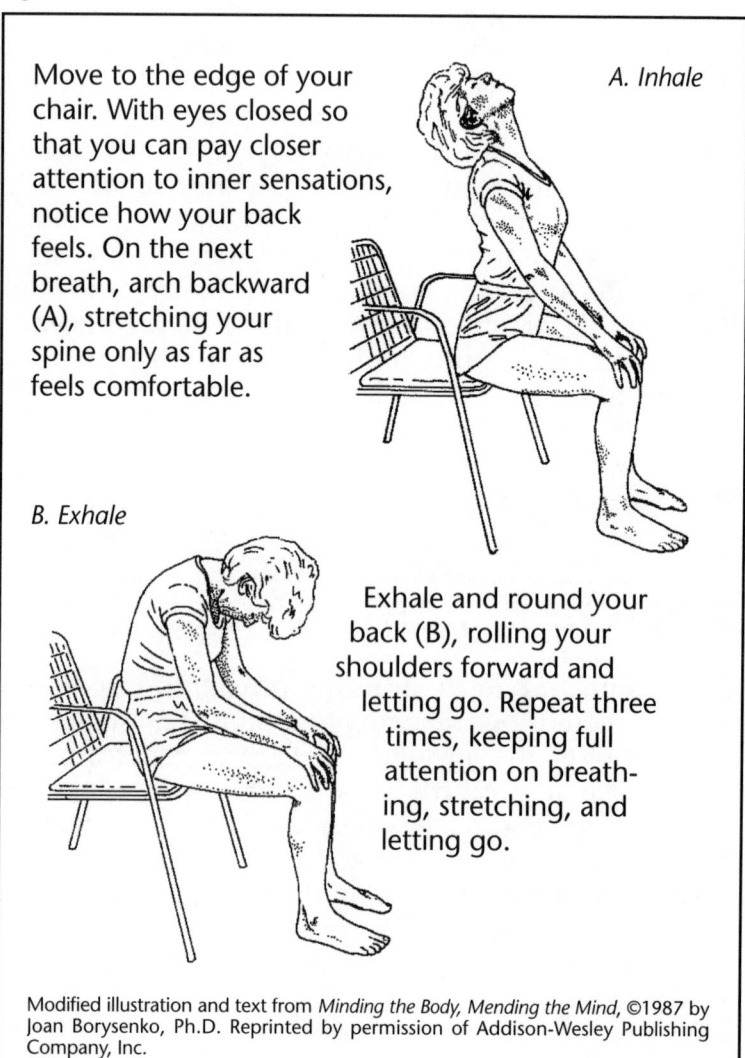

Move to the edge of your chair. With eyes closed so that you can pay closer attention to inner sensations, notice how your back feels. On the next breath, arch backward (A), stretching your spine only as far as feels comfortable.

A. Inhale

B. Exhale

Exhale and round your back (B), rolling your shoulders forward and letting go. Repeat three times, keeping full attention on breathing, stretching, and letting go.

Modified illustration and text from *Minding the Body, Mending the Mind*, ©1987 by Joan Borysenko, Ph.D. Reprinted by permission of Addison-Wesley Publishing Company, Inc.

Shoulder Shrugs

Exaggeration is a great way to show the body what it needs to know. Try to incorporate as much movement as possible when you breathe in through your nose, lifting your shoulders to your ears and rolling your shoulders back. Hold at the top of the inhalation for a count of four. Blow out through your mouth slowly and let your shoulders relax.

Fig. 2–3. Shoulder Shrugs

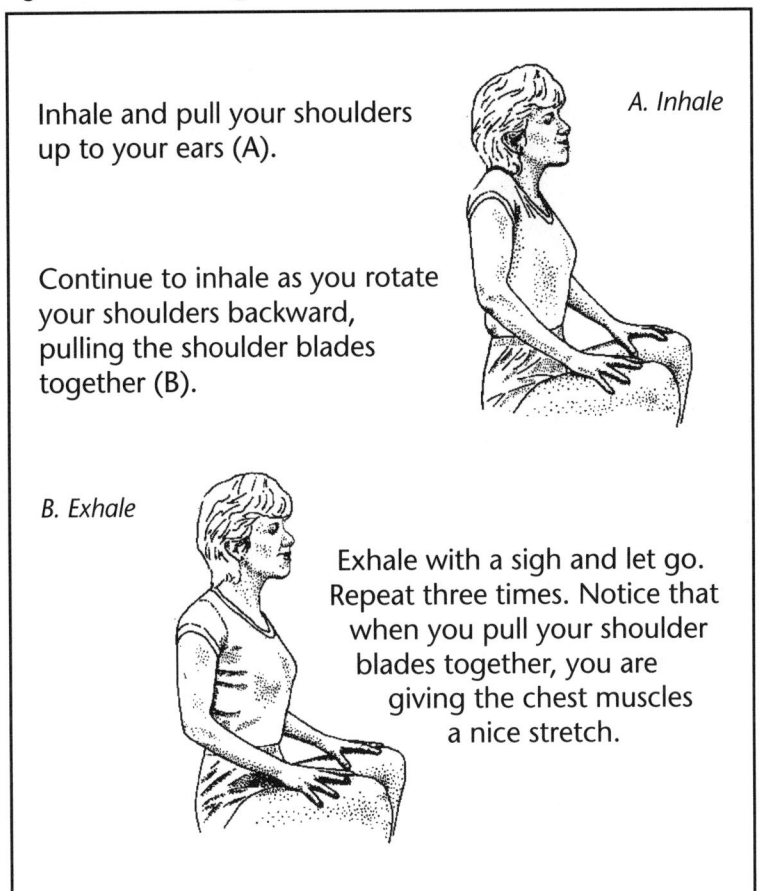

Inhale and pull your shoulders up to your ears (A).

A. Inhale

Continue to inhale as you rotate your shoulders backward, pulling the shoulder blades together (B).

B. Exhale

Exhale with a sigh and let go. Repeat three times. Notice that when you pull your shoulder blades together, you are giving the chest muscles a nice stretch.

Modified illustration and text from *Minding the Body, Mending the Mind*, ©1987 by Joan Borysenko, Ph.D. Reprinted by permission of Addison-Wesley Publishing Company, Inc.

Head Rolls

A lot of tension is stored in the musculature of the neck and shoulders. Begin the relaxation response by stretching these muscles.

Fig. 2–4. Head Rolls

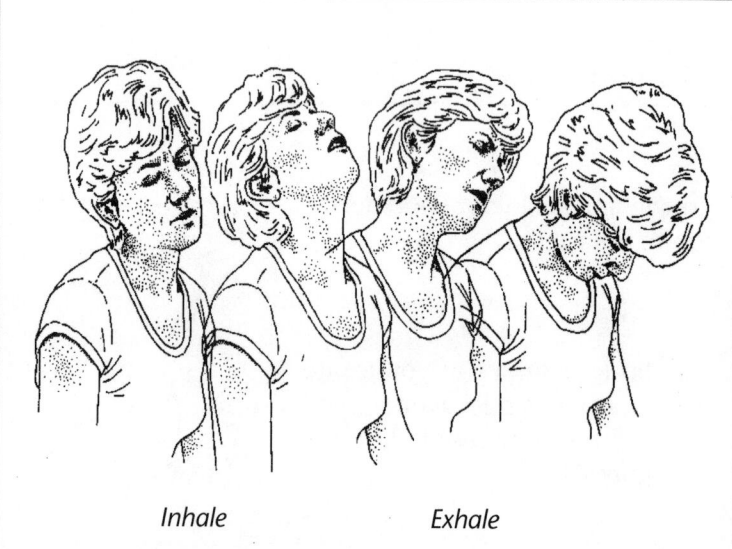

Inhale *Exhale*

Exhale as you drop your chin to your chest. Now inhale and rotate your head to the right, just letting go, letting gravity take it rather than trying to push it around. When you have rotated your head around to the back, begin to exhale. Continue the exhalation as you roll to the left and back down to the chest. Now you're ready to inhale and start over. Complete three rolls to the right and then reverse, three to the left.

Modified illustration and text from *Minding the Body, Mending the Mind*, ©1987 by Joan Borysenko, Ph.D. Reprinted by permission of Addison-Wesley Publishing Company, Inc.

Face Relaxer

Clenched teeth begins the cycle of associated muscular tension throughout the body. Relaxing your facial and neck musculature will "set the mood" to relax the rest of your body.

Barbara Meister Vitale relates in her book *Free Flight* that if you are in a stressful situation, try placing your tongue on the roof of your mouth. Some people immediately stop feeling the stress. Try it—see if you feel the difference. When you can't clench your teeth your whole face relaxes.

Fig. 2–5. Face Relaxer

Allow gravity to pull your jaw downward while relaxing your face. Hold 30 seconds. Return your jaw to its normal position. Repeat several times. Remember to always keep a small space between your upper and lower teeth to avoid gritting your teeth and clenching your jaw.

Modified illustration and text from *Minding the Body, Mending the Mind*, ©1987 by Joan Borysenko, Ph.D. Reprinted by permission of Addison-Wesley Publishing Company, Inc.

RORY'S STORY

Rory was a student I taught several years ago, before I knew about relaxation techniques in the classroom and before I realized that we all have our own unique methods of dealing with stress—particularly at school.

There could have been a special exercise for Rory: Shake your whole body while you write. I mean your whole body! Rory hated to write, so he would start his "shaker" routine as soon as he picked up a pencil. As a result, his penmanship was atrocious. No one could read it, including Rory, even after he'd worked so hard on it.

When Rory was writing, no one could work. The distracted students sitting near him would plead, "Rory, stop that!" (There were other censored versions of their requests.)

I spent my time telling the other students to ignore Rory and at least let him get started. Even though I didn't understand the behavior I was seeing at the time, I knew he wasn't doing this just to irritate us. This is what he really had to do to write!

Something had to be done. I had taken dictation before from students with severe written language problems, so I decided to try dictation with Rory. Both Rory and the other students were elated with this "solution." Rory would study math and other subjects by himself, until I could spare the time to take dictation. Sometimes, when I couldn't get to him right away, he would begin to write by himself and the shaking would start. At this point, students would say, "Mrs. Nunn, I think I can do this. Help Rory first." Or a student who was good in math would help the student I was working with so I could stop and help Rory. Rory was a good motivator for cooperative learning!

This was not the end of the problem, however. When I started to take dictation, Rory, wiggling a little in his seat beside me, grabbed my elbow and started to shake it. Not too hard, but enough so that I stopped writing because my paper was scooting around.

"Rory, what are you doing?" I asked.

"Don't know."

He sincerely seemed puzzled, but he also continued to shake my elbow, making my hand flop around. I asked him very nicely to stop and he did. But his mind stopped, too. He couldn't tell me any more answers, and that was the end of his dictation and my writing for the hour.

The same scenario was repeated the next day when Rory was dictating a creative story for English. I realized that something came unstuck in Rory's brain when he shook my elbow. In his article, "Is There a Link Between Learning Style and Neurophysiology?" (1990), Stephen Garger said that some students cannot think without moving something. Shaking was Rory's method of relaxation. It made me a little tense at first, but after a few minutes of the rhythmical movement, I noticed my shoulders were relaxing, then my whole body. And Rory's homework started getting turned in on time, for the first time ever. We all praised him, and Rory's level of frustration diminished so much, he never had to shake his whole body again.

CHAPTER 3

Taking Care of Your Own Stress

TEACHER, HEAL THYSELF

How many times in a school setting do we hear "Children First"? Before we can put children first, we need to learn how to take care of ourselves. We, as teachers, need to understand that it is not only okay to put some of our own needs first, it is absolutely essential. If we want to provide the best education possible for our students, we must learn how to keep putting something back into our teapots.

Dr. T. Berry Brazelton, the modern day Dr. Spock, was once asked to name the most important thing we could do to improve the quality of life for children. He said that if we want to help children, the first thing we had to do was help parents. He went on to explain that until parents receive adequate prenatal care, education about child rearing, ready access to day care, and time off from work to care for their children, *the children are the ones who will suffer.* I think that Dr. Brazelton would say that in a school setting, the best thing we can do for children is to help teachers first!

Teachers need to understand that it's okay to take the time to prepare their own bodies for teaching and the children's bodies for learning by breathing deeply, stretching tight muscles, and creating a comfortable environment that helps facilitate learning. Teachers need to be given information about new brain research on how to make teaching easier for the teacher and learning easier for the student.

SOMETIMES STUDENTS KNOW BEST

Dr. Gene Rooney, brain research teacher and Methodist minister, predicts that in the future teachers will be taught how to teach children to relax. I had the reverse happen to me one year. I had a *student* tell me what I had to do to reduce stress and get through the rest of the school year.

This was a particularly difficult year for me. In December, my husband died of cancer and my father died of a heart attack. I came back to school after Christmas break to a very non-supportive head teacher who said I'd missed too much school and was pulling the department down. (I had taken a family leave of absence for the month my husband was in the hospital before he died.) To make matters worse, her office was right outside my classroom and every time she walked through, she'd stop and fold her arms across her chest and appear to "observe" me.

If the students and I were laughing about something, it was difficult to keep laughing. (Her theory: if you were laughing you weren't teaching.) My stomach and bowels stayed in a fairly constant state of f/f/f. Several other teachers under her supervision seemed to experience this same state.

One of my bright, perceptive students turned, around one day when he heard her footsteps coming down the hall and said out loud: "Too bad she doesn't have to stay in her cage and listen to her own growling all day long! Maybe she'd get sick of it and quit."

My mouth fell open, the footsteps stopped, turned and went the other way. Suddenly, I couldn't help it. I started to laugh…and laugh…and laugh. It scared my students and it surprised me. When I finally stopped laughing, another student said, "Teachers have enough headaches without one of their own giving them a worse headache."

These observations from ninth-grade students flabbergasted me.

"You know what you need to do?" asked Drew, the one who'd made the "stay-in-her cage" remark. "You need to think *invisible*. She's simply invisible."

"Right, oh wise one," Carol said. "When you can hear her coming and then she stands and stares at us? We're supposed to think *invisible*?" Secretly, I agreed. I might not show anything on my face, but my insides knew differently.

"Yep." Drew was adamant. "If she's invisible, then you can't hear her and you can't see her. It'll take some work, but it will be worth it."

I thought I'd already done a very good job of covering up the negative vibrations that wafted through the corridor when she walked through.

"Don't get me wrong," Drew said, as if reading my mind. "We can see you working at it. You just haven't quite gotten there yet. Just hum a little tune when you hear her coming, never look up and we'll help.

"Remember, she simply does not exist."

It worked. It did take some effort, but it worked! One day I had my back turned to the students, getting books from the bookcase behind my desk, when Drew said, "You know, Mrs. Nunn, you are a fantastic teacher! Actually, you're the best teacher I've ever had and I think you should be teacher of the year, or given some kind of award!"

"Drew," I drawled. "That history worksheet is due to your teacher at the end of the hour and you don't need my help. So cut the blarney. It isn't going to work!" I spouted all this, never turning around.

The whole class erupted with laughter. I turned around.

"She" was just going into her office. I hadn't heard her or seen her. She had, indeed, become invisible. I stood there, looking and smiling with my students and thought: No, it hasn't really been a good year, but I've certainly learned a lot. I feel very fortunate to have learned that sometimes a source for reducing stress can come from students.

Remember

I'll end with a few key points to keep in mind about stress management and relaxation for the teacher.

1. In order for you to teach to your greatest potential, you must be physically comfortable and relaxed. You must not feel threatened.

2. Being relaxed is the best way for you to teach relaxation.

3. Any normal central nervous system can be stressed to the point where it experiences sensory defensiveness: sound becomes "too loud," touch becomes irritating, lighting becomes "too bright," and smells become noxious. Under severe stress, you may experience the same sensations that an AD/HD student with sensory motor deficit experiences on a daily basis.

4. You can "take control" by considering the senses when organizing the classroom, thereby creating a non-threatening environment:

    a) Our sense of smell is powerful. The olfactory nerve does not cross over hemispheres. It goes directly to the brain for fast transmission of information. Using natural scents such as vanilla, apple, and cinnamon will appeal to almost everyone. Do this by using plug-ins or potpourri.

    b) Adjust for bright and dim lighting to give children a choice. (Children under the f/f/f response have dilated pupils that make normal lighting "too bright.")

Knowing the impact of stress and the value of relaxation, and making these changes in your classroom, are important steps toward reducing your stress and your students' stress—and increasing learning.

CHAPTER 4

Taking Control

When Metropolitan Life Insurance Company examined 1,078 men who held the highest executive positions in "Fortune 500" companies, they found, surprisingly, that these men's mortality rate was 37 percent lower than that of other men of the same ages. Looking at other studies of executives, certain attitudes came to light that seem to offer protection against stress-related disorders. The "Fortune" executives felt a sense of purpose, and they enjoyed challenges. But, as reported in The Brain (1984), by Restak, "most important of all, they believed they were in control of their lives."

The Owner's Manual for the Brain (1994), by Howard, seconds this opinion. "How do we prevent stressors from occurring or stop them once they begin?" it asks. "The simplest answer lies in the word *control*." If we resign ourselves to the inevitability of long-term stress, it will continue to ravage our bodies. However, if we decide that we have some degree of control and can limit or prevent stressors, the effects of stress can be minimized or even eliminated.

ESTABLISHING A SENSE OF CONTROL

As a physical therapist in a hospital setting, deep breathing relaxation techniques have been invaluable to me, in part because they help patients establish a sense of control over their therapy. When I worked at Rusk Rehabilitation at the University of Missouri, some of my patients had limited ranges of motion and my job was to help them gain movement in their joints. I remember a certain stroke patient who had a "shoulder-hand syndrome." His shoulder muscles and joint structures were tight and painful and his hand was swollen, tight, and painful. After applying heat and ultrasound, I needed to passively stretch the tight muscles to gain range of motion and joint mobility. As a novice, I became frustrated when the patient "braced" himself before we began our daily ritual of passive stretching. I didn't know it at the time, but the f/f/f response was taking over. As his muscles became tighter, his pain became worse, and my job became harder.

It didn't take long for me to think I needed to try something better. I taught my patient "progressive relaxation" techniques, which began with him tensing various muscles, then relaxing them. We began at the forehead and progressed toward the toes, with the patient sequentially tensing and relaxing the muscle groups. Then we practiced the deep breathing/relaxation technique together. Now my patient could elicit a relaxed muscular state before stretching exercises started. I gave control to him and said, "When you are relaxed, let me know when you're ready for me to begin stretching." This made all the difference in the progress made. We became partners instead of adversaries.

WORKING WITH CHILDREN

When I began working in the public schools, some of my students had cerebral palsy and my job was to prevent contractures and joint deformities. The "progressive relaxation" techniques I had used in the hospital don't work well with children, mainly because they do not have a good sense of body awareness and the verbal directions often get lost, due to language processing problems.

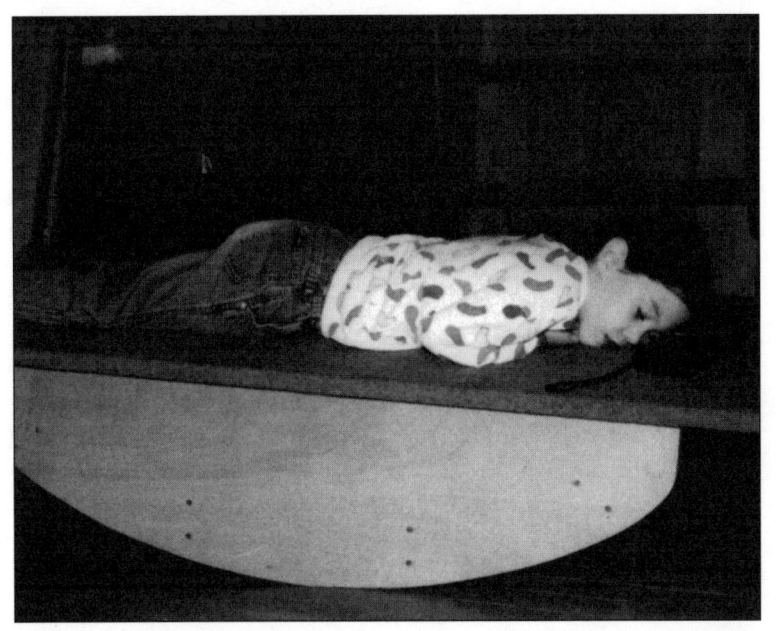

Fig. 4–1. The rocking board helps the child feel relaxed in a "total body way."

The use of a rocking board played a crucial part in my ability to teach a child how to feel relaxed in a "total body way"—right-brained approach—versus an "individual body part way"—left-brained approach. When a child lay down on the rocking board and experienced the rhythmical back and forth movement—similar to the sensation we all experienced as infants rocking in our mother's arms—relaxation was the automatic response produced by the vestibular system. This method required no language processing, awareness of body parts, or sequential thought. And, most important, the children had control over what was going to happen to them. It wasn't scary.

Later, one of my cerebral palsy students was enrolled in the behavior disordered program. The teacher, Patti Benton, noticed the deep breathing/relaxation process Jarrod was using and she remarked, "That would be good for all my students." So, we were off and running, or I should say "relaxing"! When I started out, not really knowing where I was going with this relaxation business, the program could not have been developed without the whole-hearted support of Patti Benton. She is the first behavior disorder teacher I know of in our district to use the informal classroom teaching style. If she sees that something is working to help the students, whether it's a blow-pipe or a relaxation barrel, she's for it! And when she calls her students endearing names like "angel" or "baby," the perceived threat vanishes and the f/f/f stops before it gets started.

I want to emphasize how important it is not to let the stressors get started in the first place. Remember to take deep breaths and relax those shoulders. But we also need to recognize that if stressors do start and continue, we can learn how to take control and break the anxiety cycle.

Controlling Automatic Responses

Many of the physiological effects of the f/f/f response are out of our control: they are automatic responses. It is difficult to lower your blood pressure simply by saying: "I'm going to lower my blood pressure now." Or, "I feel like I have too much adrenaline in my system, so I'm going to stop adrenaline production now!" However, there are two bodily functions, breathing and muscle relaxing, which, even though they are under control of the autonomic nervous system, can also be voluntarily controlled. By taking big, deep breaths, and by stretching out tight muscles, we can literally stop the physiologic effects of the f/f/f response.

Deep Breathing and Stretching

You learned in Chapter 2 that slow, deep breathing can help control the f/f/f response. You probably know this intuitively: how often have you told a child to slow down, take a deep breath, and start over?

But did you know that slow, deep breathing may be the first step toward changing the chemical process in the body that initiates the relaxation response? By telling

Fig. 4–2. Ball chairs are helpful to hyperactive students who need to move and learn at the same time. The student on the left is using rifle range hearing protectors to eliminate distracting noises in the classroom. The student on the right is wearing a weighted vest to help him stay calm.

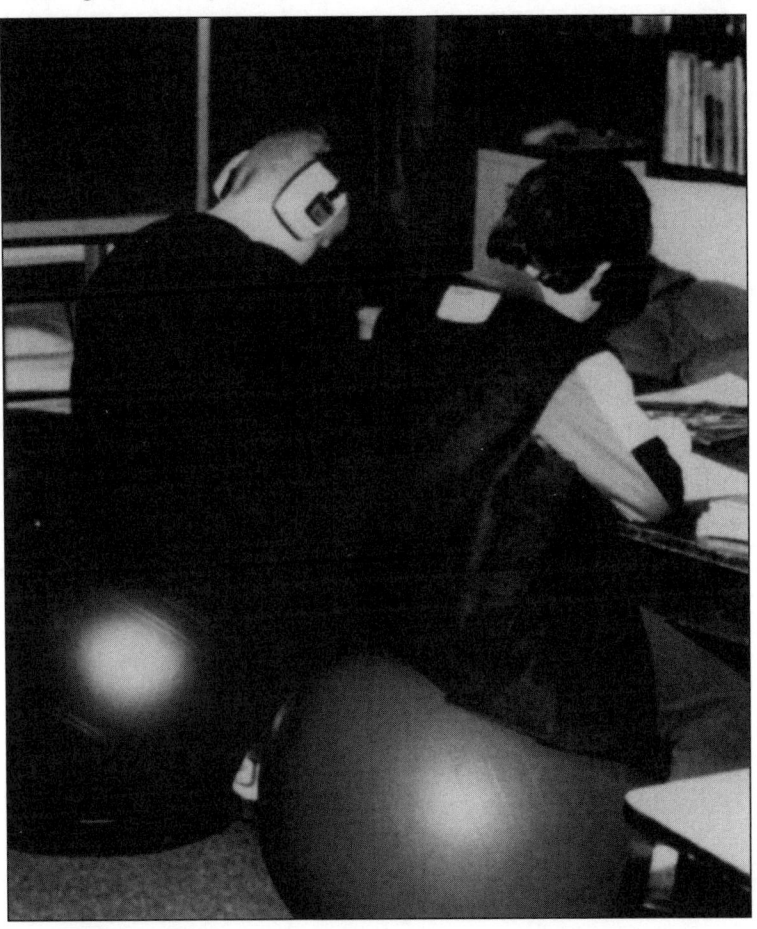

children to breathe in slowly and deeply, we are helping them maintain the proper oxygen/carbon dioxide balance in the body, so it is virtually impossible for the f/f/f response to sustain itself. Slow, deep breathing can change brain waves from an anxious "beta" state to an "alpha" state in which learning takes place most efficiently.

Muscles contract and prepare to run when the brain perceives that a threat or danger is present. During a teacher's day, many events may seem threatening: a child refusing to sit in a chair; a child refusing to work; an angry parent stopping by; a principal sitting in the classroom to evaluate you. At the end of the day, the muscles are very tight. Tight muscles put pressure on nerves, causing pain and discomfort. Pain itself is a perceived threat by the brain and more chemicals are released, causing muscles to get even tighter.

It is a vicious cycle. But the very act of stretching out muscles uses stored adrenaline, which stops the chemical process involved in the f/f/f response.

Exercise

Exercise is another way to take control and stop the f/f/f response. Reports show that, within a period of one second following a traumatic event (a near accident, the death of a loved one, a domestic fight), the brain releases harmful "stress" chemicals that remain in the body for at least twenty-four hours. These chemicals literally stop the learning process. The best way to dissipate or use up these chemicals is by vigorous exercise. Exercise restores the chemical balance in the body by stimulating the brain's production of the hormone norepinephrine, which is directly related to emotional stability and the production of endorphins (substances that act as natural opiates to produce a "runner's high.") So when you're feeling stressed out, remember to exercise.

In fact, after writing and rereading these last two paragraphs, I've become anxious. I think I need to take control, turn the computer off, stop sitting on my chemicals, and go for a long walk with my dog.

CHAPTER 5

Shifting Gears/Alertness

If we, as adults, understand what methods we use to change or maintain alertness levels, then we will be able to assist our students with the same. This understanding will reduce the stress levels of both teacher and student.

At a recent workshop for teachers on "The Brain and Learning," the lecturer, Dr. Gene Rooney, said that one of the best lessons we can teach children is how to "shift gears" from an f/f/f state to a state of relaxed alertness. Being in a chronic state of stress is like stepping on the gas and putting on the brake at the same time.

USING SENSORY INPUT

How Does Your Engine Run? (1994), by Williams and Shellenberger, is an innovative book that teaches us how to relieve stress and learn better by using sensory input in our daily lives. The primary focus of the book is helping children learn to monitor, maintain, and change their level of alertness so that it is appropriate to a situation or task. The "Alertness Program" was designed for children with learning disabilities but can be adapted for all children, from preschool age through adulthood. The program offers specific activities that can be used for self -regulation.

How Does Your Engine Run? teaches us how to observe our bodies and understand the mostly subconscious techniques we use to change our bodies' "alertness levels." In other words, we can use our senses to calm ourselves down or pep ourselves up, depending on what the situation calls for. Williams and Shellenberger say:

> If your body is like a car engine, sometimes you may feel like your engine is running in high speed; you may find it difficult to pay attention; to sit quietly in your seat; or get your work completed. When your engine is in low speed, you also may find it hard to concentrate; you may daydream easily, or feel like a couch potato. When you are in the "just right" place, it's usually easier to pay attention, to get your work done, and to have fun. (p. A-45)

CHANGING HOW ALERT YOU FEEL

There are a number of methods you can use to change your engine speed from high or low to "just right". The following list gives examples of how you and your students can use your senses to change your level of alertness.

CHANGE HOW ALERT YOU FEEL

1. **Put Something in Your Mouth**
   - Eat hard candy (sugarless if you want).
   - Eat crunchy food: pretzels, popcorn, nuts, apples.
   - Eat chewy food: gum (one or more pieces), raisins, bagels, chunks of cheese.
   - Eat sour food: pickles, sour candy.
   - Eat sweet food: fruit or candy.
   - Drink from a straw: use an "exercise bottle" to drink liquids such as milkshakes, "Slurpies" (partially thaw a frozen drink), or other drinks.
   - Try a combination such as trail mix (crunchy, chewy, sweet), Starburst (chewy, sweet, and tart), or chips dipped into salsa (crunchy and spicy).
   - Take slow deep breaths.

2. **Move (Try moving before you need to concentrate on a task.)**
   - Do isometrics (push arms against a wall or push hands together).
   - Walk quickly.
   - Run up and down steps.
   - Do an errand for a teacher.
   - Shake your head quickly.
   - Roll your neck slowly in circular motion.
   - Jump up and down, or try to jump to touch a door frame.
   - Play sports: basketball, swimming, baseball, Frisbee, etc.
   - Do aerobics with a group or at home to music.
   - Dance.
   - Doodle on paper (if it doesn't distract you).
   - Use a therapy ball.

3. **Touch**
   - Try holding and fidgeting with a Koosh ball, paper clips, rubber bands, straw, jewelry, or clay.

—continued

- Rub gently or vigorously on your skin or clothing.
- Take a cool shower or warm bath.
- Wash your face with a cold or hot wash cloth.
- Pet or play with an animal.
- Hold or lean against a stuffed animal or large pillows.

4. Look
- Put bright lights on in room if you are in low speed.
- Dim the lights if you are in high speed.
- Clear off the table where you're working if objects distract you.
- Watch fish in an aquarium.
- Read a book or look at a magazine.

5. Listen
- Listen to classical (and similar) music (even, slow beat).
- Listen to hard rock (and similar) music (loud bass, uneven beat).
- Use a personal cassette player if the music bothers someone else.
- Avoid loud, noisy places if you are in high speed or trying to concentrate.

Developed by Williams & Shellenberger, © 1994, TherapyWorks, Inc. Reprinted with permission.

SENSORY MOTOR PREFERENCE

What does your body do to maintain alertness or shift gears? The "Sensory Motor Preference Checklist for Adults" was developed to help adults recognize what strategies their own nervous systems employ to attain an appropriate state of alertness. When you have a chance to examine your own habits more closely, you will be fascinated with how you subconsciously maintain your own alertness levels. Have fun finding your own regulatory mechanisms in the list below:

SENSORY-MOTOR PREFERENCE CHECKLIST
(for adults)

Mark the items below that you use to increase ↑ or to decrease ↓ your state of alertness. You might mark both ↑ ↓ on some items. Others you might not use at all.

Something in Your Mouth (Oral Motor Input)

_____	Drink a milkshake	_____	Chew gum
_____	Suck on hard candy	_____	Crunch on nuts/pretzels/chips
_____	Crunch or suck on ice pieces	_____	Bite on nails/cuticle
_____	Tongue in cheek movements	_____	Eat popcorn/cut up vegetables
_____	"Chew" on pencil/pen	_____	Eat chips and a spicy dip
_____	Chew on coffee swizzle sticks	_____	Smoke cigarettes
_____	Take slow, deep breaths	_____	Chew on buttons, sweatshirt strings, or collars
_____	Suck, lick, bite on your lips or the inside of your cheeks	_____	Whistle while you work
_____	Drink carbonated drink	_____	Drink coffee/tea
_____	Eat a cold popsicle	_____	Drink hot cocoa or warm milk
_____	Eat a pickle	_____	Other: _____

Move (Vestibular Input)

_____	"Doodle" while listening	_____	Sit with crossed legs and bounce one slightly
_____	Rock in a rocking chair	_____	Run/jog
_____	Shift or "squirm" in a chair	_____	Ride bike
_____	Push chair back on two legs	_____	Tap toe, heel or foot
_____	Aerobic exercise	_____	Dance
_____	Isometrics/lift weights	_____	Tap pencil/pen
_____	Rock own body slightly	_____	Yard work
_____	Scrub kitchen floor	_____	Stretch/shake body parts
_____	Roll neck and head slowly	_____	Other: _____

—continued

Touch (Tactile Input)

_____ Twist own hair
_____ Move keys or coins in pocket with your hand
_____ Cool shower
_____ Warm bath
_____ Receive a massage
_____ Pet a dog or cat
_____ Drum fingers or pencil on table
_____ Rub gently on skin/clothes

Fidget with the following:
_____ A straw
_____ Paper clips
_____ Cuticle/nails
_____ Pencil/pen
_____ Earring or necklace
_____ Phone cord while talking
_____ Put fingers near mouth, eye, or nose
_____ Other: _____

Look (Visual Input)

_____ open window shades after a boring movie in a classroom
_____ watch a fireplace
_____ watch a fish tank
_____ watch sunset/sunrise
_____ watch "oil and water" toys

How do you react to:
_____ dim lighting
_____ fluorescent lighting
_____ sunlight through bedroom window when sleeping
_____ rose colored room
_____ a "cluttered desk" when you need to concentrate

Listen (Auditory Input)

_____ listen to classical music
_____ listen to hard rock
_____ listen to others hum
_____ work in quiet room
_____ work in noisy room
_____ sing or talk to self

How do you react to:
_____ scratch on a chalkboard
_____ "squeak" of a mechanical pencil
_____ fire siren
_____ waking to an unusual noise
_____ dog barking (constantly)

Questions to Ponder:

Review this sensory-motor preference checklist. Think about what you do in a small, subtle manner to maintain an alertness level that a child with a less mature nervous system may need to do in a larger, more intense way.

> Notice which types of sensory input are comforting to your nervous system and which types of sensory input bother your nervous system. Are your items clustered in a certain category of sensory input?
>
> Consider how often (frequency), how long (duration), how much (intensity), and with what rhythm (fast, slow, uneven, or even) you use these inputs to change your state of alertness.
>
> From *How Does Your Engine Run?* Developed by Williams & Shellenberger, © 1992, TherapyWorks, Inc. Reprinted with permission.

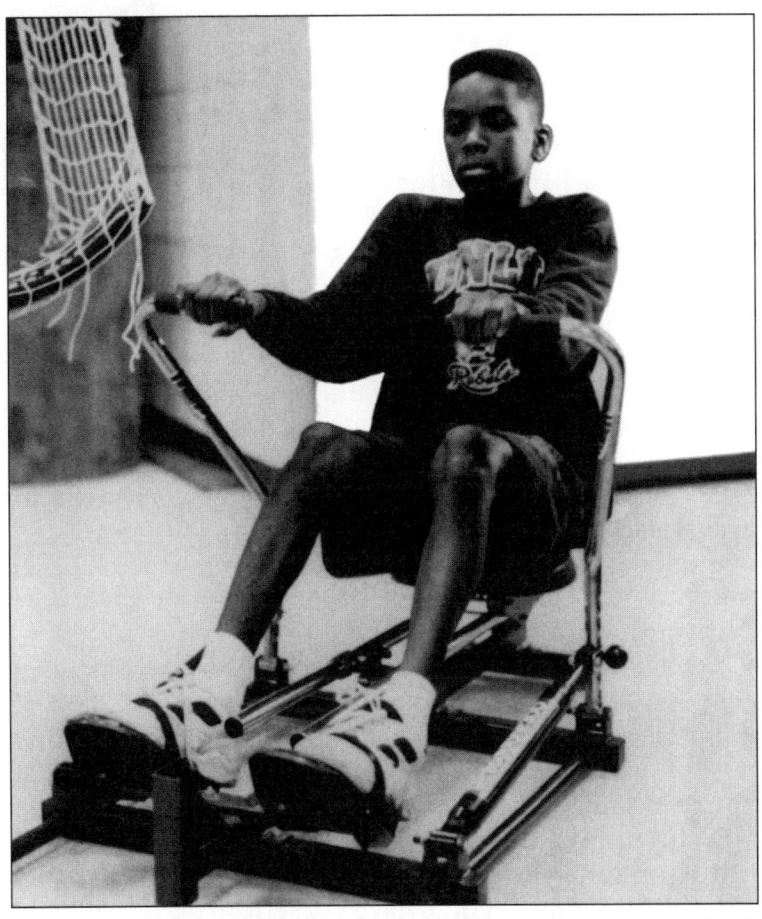

Fig. 5–1. Exercise produces the relaxation response, alters alertness levels and relieves stress. AD/HD students who experience these benefits can use exercise for self control. What a wonderful life skill!

SLOWING DOWN

When I began observing my own behavior, I found that my speed of movement was an external indicator of my internal state. As a physical therapist for the school system, I work at several different schools and I noticed that at one particular school, the staff actually moves at a faster pace. I found myself getting pulled into the "stream of movement" and began walking faster, talking faster, and reaching for things more quickly.

I also began noticing the difference this kind of fast, jerky movement had on my thought process. I began feeling pressured. I didn't really enjoy what I was doing, and I couldn't figure out why. I found it harder and somewhat irritating when I went through the deep breathing/relaxation part of my treatment program with the first student of the day. I kept wanting to say: "Hurry up and relax! We've got to get going!"

During the relaxation time for the second student, I began to really relax and enjoy the three minutes it took to listen to the musical selection the student had chosen. The feeling of being pressured went away and I began enjoying what I was doing again.

One day it dawned on me what was happening: the atmosphere in this one school was stressful. Once I realized this, I tried to prepare myself to stay relaxed when I was there. It took me quite a while to figure out that for me the key to staying calm was connected with my own speed of movement. When I told myself to "stay calm," but continued to walk and talk fast, I couldn't stay calm. The old sensation of pressure returned. I began practicing walking and talking at a slower speed and noticed an improvement in my inner calmness. ("Slower speed" only means "not rushed" speed. Certainly you don't have to move in slow motion!)

I also noticed that I began feeling like I was out of sync with the other faculty members and worried that they might think that I didn't have enough work to do! What a ridiculous thought! Just because I was able to reduce my anxiety level shouldn't mean that I was being less productive than my cohorts. In fact, I knew that my calm state of mind was definitely helping me be more effective with my own students.

As I began to understand the f/f/f response, this personal phenomenon made a lot of sense. As soon as my body began picking up speed by walking fast and jerky, the autonomic nervous system began interpreting a sense of "danger." The other elements of the f/f/f response began kicking in to assist in "survival": shallow breathing, increased heart rate, increased adrenaline, and so on. By slowing down (probably only by a nanosecond), I was able to keep this process from self-initiating. How simple!

So, do yourself a favor and *slow down*!

CHAPTER 6

Self-Observation

Self-observation is that wonderful ability of looking at ourselves and being able to figure out what we need to keep us going in this world.

Learning to self-observe and understand how your engine runs and what it needs to change speeds is a major stress reducer in itself. The following stories show how important self-observation is and how it can work. Let's start with Vincent, Janet's student:

VINCENT'S STORY

Vincent is one of my star relaxation students. One day, I was visiting Vincent's home with the teacher of his behavior disordered classroom, Ms. Benton. We were having a conference and when Vincent's mom saw one of my goals: Be able to breathe deeply and relax to improve classroom behavior, she said, "Oh! Now I know where it's coming from."

Vincent's mom had come home one afternoon to find Vincent's baby-sitter, Tammy, puzzled by what had just happened. Vincent had run into the house and slammed the door, with expletives flowing about that stupid kid down the block who "wouldn't let me play baseball! I could just kill him!" With this, he ran up the stairs to his room.

Tammy waited for the explosion that usually came next when Vincent was upset: books being thrown, doors being kicked, and the wall being beaten. But this time there was silence. She waited for the bomb to drop. No bomb. Tammy became curious and tiptoed up the steps. Vincent's door was not closed all the way and Tammy peeked in. She saw Vincent doing the strangest thing. He was standing in front of his mirror taking big breaths in and blowing out.

Tommy told Vincent's mom that "Vincent is one strange kid."

We were elated with his "strangeness."

MS. BENTON'S STORY

Vincent's teacher, Ms. Benton, had seen me working with her behavior disordered students, doing deep breathing/relaxation techniques for self-calming. When they were able to "take three big breaths" instead of getting mad or out of control, they were awarded a "Super Star Award" in front of the class, with recognition by the principal. If they were able to coach a friend to "take three big breaths" to keep from getting into a fight, an award was in order for both students.

One day Ms. Benton told me she would be late the following morning since she had to get her blood drawn for some routine tests. She said she dreaded going because her veins were so hard to find. It was not uncommon for her to endure twelve or thirteen sticks before the nurse had success.

I told her to remember to take three big breaths and try to stay "loose as a goose" to see if that would help.

The next day Ms. Benton arrived in the classroom with a Band-Aid at the crook of her arm and a bigger-than-the-Band-Aid smile on her face. She told her students: "I kept telling myself to breathe and stay relaxed. And it worked!" The nurse only had to stick her once.

The students were so proud of their teacher, they gave her a big round of applause and, more important, the "Super Star Award!" (She waived the recognition by the principal!)

JAKE'S STORY

Sometimes students know what they need in order to learn. We simply have to learn to listen to them. Jake seemed as if he were moving underwater. Every movement took so much energy, so much thought. He "spaced out" a lot. I heard complaints from all his teachers, saying the same things repeatedly: "He isn't listening," or "He isn't trying," or "He's not getting his work finished." (This same student programmed fancy calculators for students and sometimes for teachers.)

One day I had my oscillating fan going. Besides cooling them, the hum was soothing to a lot of my students. This particular day, Jake, who rarely talked said, "I like that fan when the breeze hits my face. It's like it's keeping me awake."

I was surprised. "You mean like when someone gets sleepy driving a car and opens a window for some air on their face?"

"Yeah!" Jake actually got excited. "If I could have that fan on my face all the time, I think I could get more of my work done."

I heard groans from the other students, mostly say-ing how Jake wanted to hog the fan. But I suspected differently.

Jake brought his own clip-on fan from home and used it summer and winter. He needed this to keep his alertness level "just right." I sat him next to a student who was hyperactive and who loved and was calmed by the sound of the fan. A double benefit. Self-preservation—as well as self-observation—is a wonderful thing! If Jake hadn't mentioned how the breeze from the fan affected him, it would have been the last thing I would have thought of to help him with his work.

At the end of the year, I had the students answer this question briefly, as a sort of "self-observation" test. The question: What have I learned about myself this year?

Before I tell you Jake's answer, I'd like to preface it with a small incident that had happened at the beginning of school. The first day was over and everyone had cleared out. But there was Jake, sitting with his back against a locker, a pile of books in his lap and an expression on his face that I'll never forget. I remember thinking that he was sick.

"Oh, Jake," I asked, "Did you have a bad day?"

"Why?" he asked.

I was caught off guard. "Your face, it looks so tight and you looked wiped out."

Jake didn't smile. He said simply, "Mrs. Nunn, I always look like this."

So you can imagine my pleasure when I read Jake's answer to the question. He said, "I used to worry so much about what I was going to say when people talked to me or asked me questions. Now I don't worry about it

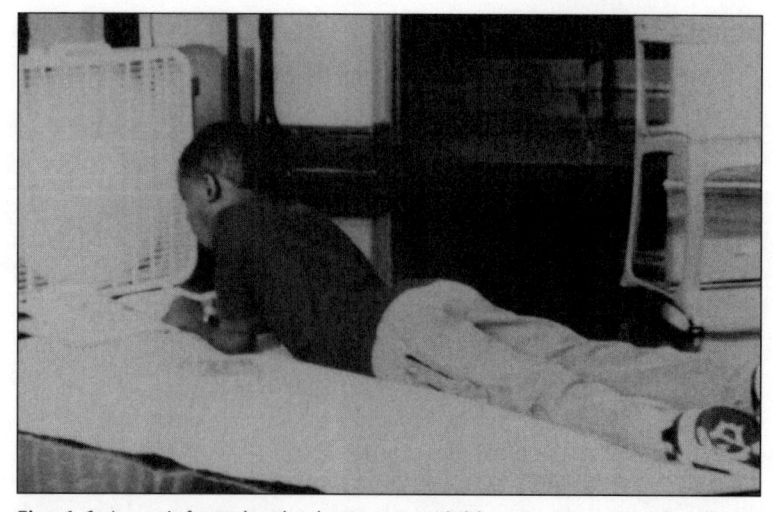

Fig. 6–1. In an informal style classroom, a child may use a prone on elbows position to read, which is an excellent way to build scapular strength. The blanket defines space for a child with poor body awareness and the fan drowns out distracting noises for the auditorily sensitive child.

so much. I just pretty much say what I want to, and if it sounds stupid, I don't care so much."

Learning to observe ourselves and know what we need, physically and mentally, is hard work. But what a blessing it is to us forever, once we begin to figure it out.

I was one of the leaders of TREND, a drug-free group, and Jake's father organized a float trip for several members that summer. I told them I wasn't crazy about float trips because I had been dumped so often, but if they put someone in the canoe with me who promised not to let me "dump," I'd give it a try. Jake said he'd take care of it and his Dad said I was in good hands. I was a little leery. Jake didn't move real fast, and I remembered the Missouri rivers and their strong currents and wondered what I was letting myself in for.

Sure enough, we almost got caught on some rocks in a fairly swift current, with hanging tree limbs trying to wrestle us out of the canoe. I yelled, a little panic-stricken, "Oh, Jake, I don't like this!"

And Jake, in his dry way, who had been telling me when to paddle and what to do, said, "I'm not crazy about this myself." But he told me to keep calm and do what he said, and we'd come out all right.

We did. And I couldn't help but think (after our crisis was over) how what Jake had said about keeping calm and we'd come out all right applied so much to teaching.

MITCH'S STORY

Mitch was the student I had sitting next to Jake for the soothing sound of the fan. He would come to class so tightly wired that even after our relaxation breathing and stretching exercises, he needed something more.

He came flying into the classroom one day, upset over a grade by one teacher, a slight another student had "done to me" and something his dad had said to him the night before. "I'm so tight," he said, "that I feel like the top of my head could blow off!" And without realizing he was doing it, the whole time he was telling me about everything, he was flipping one of those hacky sack balls with his knees as high as he could, pacing up and down behind his desk.

In a very short time, he said, "Whew! I feel better." And he sat down and started working. From then on, Mitch would get to class a few minutes early and start hacky-sacking and letting off verbal steam if he had to. His working habits and disposition improved greatly.

I was interested and pleased at the answer Mitch gave to the self-observation test at the end of the year. Mitch said he'd learned how not to be so rigid. That he'd figured out he could relax some and live with himself—and his Dad!— better.

PART II

Focus on the Student

We must believe that every young child's basic desire is to learn new things and be praised for that effort. When a child fails to learn as quickly as might be expected, or when a child appears to be "not trying hard enough," it is our duty as educators to analyze the child's learning style and sensory motor development to discover how he or she learns and to adapt our teaching to that style.

—Janet Gallaher

CHAPTER 7

Learning Styles

For the last twenty years or more, educators have been aware that each individual learns in a unique way. An individual's learning style is as unique as his or her fingerprint. What facilitates learning for one individual may totally block the learning process for another. David Hunt, Kenneth Dunn, and Joseph Rensulli have spearheaded the learning styles theory movement.

"Learning styles" refers to a method of teaching and learning that is the single most researched subject in the history of education. It has been researched by 60 institutions of higher learning and includes all ages—kindergarten through college—and all levels of ability, including gifted, average, underachieving, at-risk, and drop-out populations.

According to Dr. Rita Dunn, research on learning styles explains why certain children perform well in school when their siblings don't. It also shows how boys' styles differ from girls' and the differences between youngsters who learn to read easily and those who have more difficulty.

But more important than all this documentation is the fact that knowing learning styles provides clear directions for how to teach individuals by using the right styles, or how to teach them to teach themselves by capitalizing on their personal strengths. And when we can do that, we reduce stress and increase learning.

IDENTIFYING LEARNING STYLES

A variety of assessment tools have been developed to help teachers understand different learning styles and to help teachers, parents, and students find out about their own learning styles, strengths, and weaknesses. These tools may run the gamut—from informally considering and evaluating our own methods of understanding and remembering new and difficult material, to the very thorough and standardized Learning Styles Inventory by Dunn, Dunn and Price. Many experienced teachers who have studied their own learning style and several testing instruments may be able to quickly assess a student's preferred learning style by observing the student in the classroom.

We would like to describe three learning styles assessment tools.

Learning Self-Assessment

The Learning Self-Assessment (developed by the University College of the Cariboo Student Program in 1991) is a list of 10 questions, with 3 options to complete a sentence that seems "most typical of you." The results will tell you if you are primarily auditory, visual, or kinesthetic in your learning and self-expression.

There are ten incomplete sentences and three choices for completing each sentence. Some of the choices contain more than one option. If any one of these options seems typical of you, score that answer. All of the options do not have to apply to you.

Score the three choices by rating (3) to the answer most typical of you, (2) to your second choice, and (1) to the answer least typical of you.

LEARNING SELF-ASSESSMENT

1. **When I learn something new, I usually:**

    a. _____ want someone to explain it to me.

    b. _____ want to read about it in a book or magazine.

    c. _____ want to try it out, take notes, or make a model of it.

2. **At a party, most of the time I like to:**

    a. _____ listen and talk to two or three people at once.

    b. _____ see how everyone looks and watch the people.

    c. _____ dance, play games, or take part in some activities.

3. **If I were helping with a musical show, I would most likely:**

    a. _____ write the music, sing the songs, or play the accompaniment.

    b. _____ design the costumes, paint the scenery, or work the lighting effects.

    c. _____ make the costumes, build the sets, or take an acting role.

4. **When I am angry, my first reaction is to:**

    a. _____ tell people off, laugh, joke, or talk it over with someone.

    b. _____ blame myself or someone else, daydream about taking revenge, or keep it inside.

    c. _____ make a fist, tense my muscles, take it out on something else, hit or throw things.

5. **A happy event I would like to have is:**

    a. _____ hearing thunderous applause for my speech or music.

    b. _____ photographing the prized picture of a sensational newspaper story.

    c. _____ achieving the fame of being first in a physical activity such as dancing, acting, surfing, or sports event.

    —continued

6. **I prefer a teacher to:**

   a. ____ use the lecture method with informative explanations and discussions.

   b. ____ write on the chalkboard, use visual aids, and assign readings.

   c. ____ require posters, models, or inservice practice, and some in class.

7. **I know that I talk with:**

   a. ____ different tones of voice.

   b. ____ my eyes and facial expressions.

   c. ____ my hands and gestures.

8. **If I had to remember an event so that I could record it later, I would choose to:**

   a. ____ tell it aloud to someone, or hear an audio tape recording or a song about it.

   b. ____ see pictures of it, or read a description.

   c. ____ replay it in some practice rehearsal using movements such as dance, play-acting, or drill.

9. **When I cook something new, I like to:**

   a. ____ have someone tell me the directions—a friend or television show.

   b. ____ read the recipe and judge by how it looks.

   c. ____ use many pots and dishes, stir often, and taste test.

10. **In my free time, I like to:**

    a. ____ listen to the radio, talk on the telephone, or attend a musical event.

    b. ____ go to the movies, watch television, or read a magazine or book.

    c. ____ get some exercise, go for a walk, play games or make things.

Total all "a" choices ____**Auditory**   Your score _____

Total all "b" choices ____**Visual**   Your score _____

Total all "c" choices ____**Kinesthetic** Your score _____

Each score will range from 10 to 30; together they will total 60. The auditory score means that you learn and express yourself through sounds and hearing. The visual score means that you enjoy learning and expressing yourself with your eyes, seeing things written, colors, and imageries. The kinesthetic score means that you learn and express yourself through physical and muscular activities and practice.

If the scores are within four points of each other, you have a mixed modality, which means that you process information in any sensory modality with balanced ease.

If there are five points or more between any of the scores, you have a relative strength in that modality as compared to the others. You may have two modalities that seem stronger than the other one. This means that you learn more easily and express yourself more naturally in the modality with the larger score(s).

There are, of course, no right or wrong choices of sensory modalities. This checklist simply reveals the sensory modalities that you have learned to depend on and enjoy the most. You can practice improving your skill in any modality, with the goal of achieving a mixed and balanced modality of sensory strengths.

Developed by University College of the Cariboo, Student Success Programs.

The C.I.T.E. Learning Styles Instrument

The C.I.T.E. Learning Styles Instrument (developed by Babich, Burdine, Albright, and Randol at the Wichita Public Schools—Murdock Teacher Center), is a questionnaire consisting of 45 items that are scored on a scale of 1 to 4 from "most like me" to "least like me." Numerical results yield scores that indicate the subject's "Major Learning Style," "Minor Learning Style," and "Negligible Use Style." The information is divided into nine areas: Visual Language, Visual Numerical, Auditory Language, Auditory Numerical, Social-Individual, Social-Group, Expressiveness-Oral, Expressiveness-Written, and Kinesthetic Tactile. It includes a checklist for planning teaching strategies.

The Learning Styles Inventory

The Learning Styles Inventory (by Dunn, Dunn and Price) surveys individuals' preferences in each of twenty-two different areas. It is a comprehensive approach to identifying how students prefer to function, learn, concentrate, and perform during educational activities in the following areas:

- *Environment:* sound, temperature, light, and design (formal or informal);
- *Emotionality:* motivation, responsibility persistence, and the need for either structure or flexibility;
- *Sociological needs:* learning alone, with peers, with adults, and/or in several ways;
- *Physical needs:* perceptual preferences, time of day, intake, and mobility.

Questions concerning each of the areas are presented, and selected responses tend to reveal highly personalized preferences that represent the way in which the individual prefers to study or concentrate. The completed questionnaire is sent to The Price Systems where it is scored. (There is a fee per student.) The student receives a printout that shows his or her relative preferences in all 22 areas.

LEARNING STYLES INVENTORY

1. **Noise Level**—Quiet or Sound. Some people need quiet; others may need background noise.
2. **Light**—Low or Bright. Some people need very bright light; others are bothered by bright light and need low lighting.
3. **Temperature**—Cool or Warm. Some students "can't think" when they feel hot; others can't think when it's cold.
4. **Design**—Informal or Formal. Some students need bean bags, the floor, pillows, or carpeting. Some do better seated on steel, wooden, or plastic chairs.
5. **Motivation**—Some students are highly motivated to achieve; others are not.
6. **Persistence**—Some students are inclined to take breaks and complete assignments later; others do their work all at once.
7. **Responsibility**—Some students don't work because they don't like being told what to do; others' responsibility is related to following through because the teacher asks them to.
8. **Structure**—Some students want a great deal of structure; others prefer very little.
9. **Peer-Orientation**—Some people work better by themselves; some work best with others.
10. **Authority Figure Present**—Some people feel better when someone with authority or special knowledge is present.
11. **Prefers Learning in Several Ways**—Some people may learn easily alone and with other people present, or they may need variety as opposed to routines.
12. **Auditory Preferences**—Some students prefer listening to verbal instruction such as a lecture, discussion, or recording.
13. **Visual Preferences**—Some students can close their eyes and visually recall what they have read or seen earlier.
14. **Tactile Preferences**—These students need to underline, take notes, keep their hands busy.

—continued

> 15. **Kinesthetic Preferences**—These learners require whole body movement or active involvement. (Acting, puppetry, and drama; building, interviewing, and playing.)
> 16. **Intake Preferences**—Some students eat, drink, chew, or bite objects while concentrating; others prefer no intake until after they have finished studying.
> 17. **Functions Best in Evening/Morning**—Evening and morning are on a continuum; if a score falls below 40, the student tends to be an evening person; if the score is above 60, the student prefers to learn in the morning.
> 18. **Functions Best in Late Morning**—Energy curve is highest in late morning; learning preference is for this time of day.
> 19. **Functions Best in Afternoon**—Energy curve is highest in afternoon; learning preference is for this time of day.
> 20. **Parent Figure Motivated**—These students want to achieve to please their parents.
> 21. **Teacher Motivated**—These students want to learn and complete their assignments because their teachers will be pleased with their efforts.
> 22. **Mobility**—How still can a person sit and for how long? Some people need frequent "breaks" and must move about; others can sit for hours while engaged in learning, particularly if they are interested in the task.

Knowing about learning styles reduces stress and enables teachers to work effectively with students who might otherwise be misdiagnosed with AD/HD or another learning disability. In "Survey of Research on Learning Styles" (1989), Dunn, Beaudry, and Clavas point out the importance of understanding the need for movement:

> One element of learning style is the need for physical activity, and a review of this research reveals how this need can be confused with other, more alarming diagnosis. For example, Fadley and Hosler (1979) noted that children often were referred to psychologists because of their consistent hyperactivity; their teachers complained

that such youngsters were unable to sit quietly and pay attention during lessons. Those psychologists reported that most students sent to them were not at all clinically hyperactive; instead, they were normal children in need of movement. In addition, the less interested they were in the lesson, the more mobility the children required. (p. 175)

Fig. 7–1. A stationary bicycle can be used in the classroom by those students who require mobility in order to learn. Relaxation tapes (classical music or instrumental music) are used to block out distracting sounds.

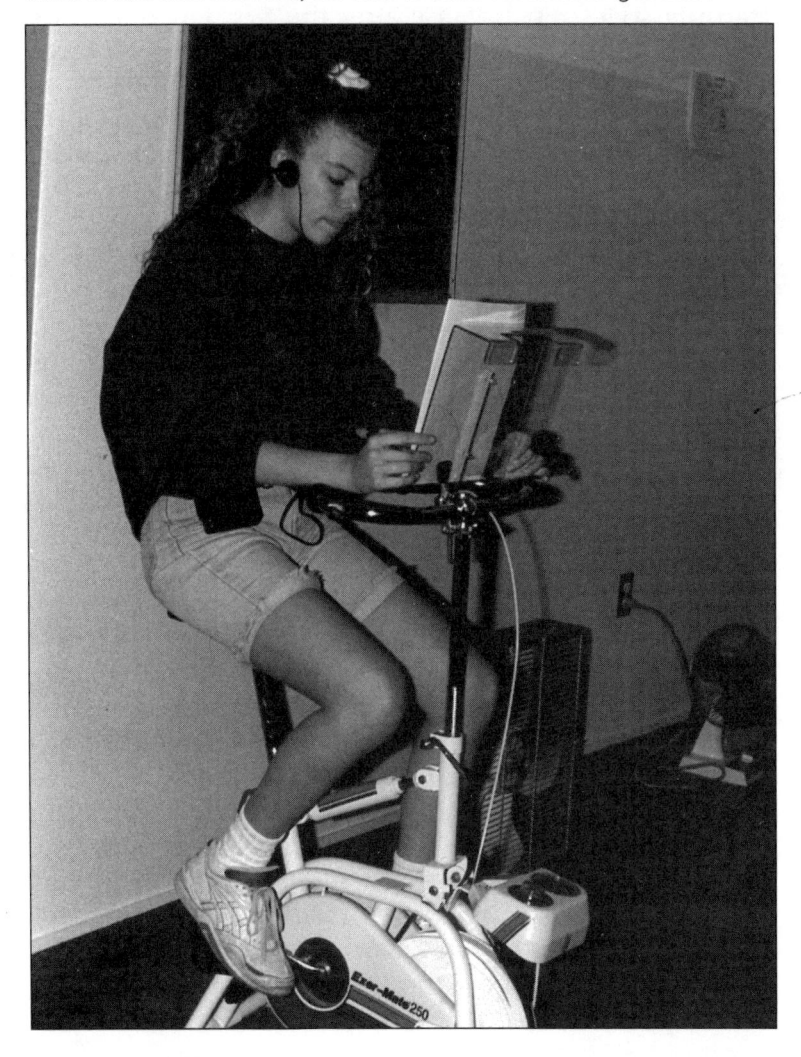

Gary's Story

Parents as well as teachers can be fooled by a student's need for mobility into thinking that the student is hyperactive. I had a student who was driving both his mother and me crazy. No matter how I tried to teach Gary, no matter what learning style I tried or what test I gave him to discover his learning style, Gary was failing. Everything! And Gary was not a low ability student. (I found out later that he just marked anything on the learning styles test because after the first few questions, he couldn't seem to concentrate on the rest. And if I read it to him, it really didn't work.)

By accident, something his mother said to me over the phone when we were discussing one of Gary's many "F" classes, provided the clue to Gary's learning style—his only learning style.

Gary's mother complained that when she sent him to his room to study, all he did was kick his soccer ball into the wall with no pictures—but he continued to lie to her and say he was studying. "He never sits at his desk and studies, and I can hear that soccer ball whomping against the wall when he has the nerve to tell me he is studying!"

"Does it whomp all the time?" I asked, beginning to get excited.

She hesitated, thinking. "Nooooo, he quits a little while when he says he's reading, but then he stops reading and starts kicking that ball again."

"That's it!" I yelled. "Make sure he reads all those notes on history tonight and let's see how he does on his test tomorrow, and whatever you do, don't tell him to sit at his desk. Let him keep kicking the soccer ball."

Of course, Gary's mother thought I was crazier than her son by now, but what she didn't realize was that she'd just told me Gary was a mobility learner. A very unconventional mobility learner. Read some...kick some...read some...kick some...digest what he'd read...kick the ball some more. I could hardly wait to see how he did on his test.

Gary made 98%! And although he couldn't kick a soccer ball in the classroom every day, at least his mother knew he was indeed doing his homework at night and his teachers now knew to send Gary on lots of errands to and from the office.

Because of the understanding of his learning styles modality, Gary is now allowed to take the tests at school in a large commons room where he can walk around. He's now making A's and B's.

A modern, mobility, modality miracle, wouldn't you say?

Thank goodness for the Dunn and Dunn research model that makes us aware of all the learning modalities. The Dunn and Dunn model is the only one we know of that acknowledges the importance of both environmental and biological differences in learning. The model takes into account the biological differences in learning styles: some people may be able to use any one of the modalities as effectively as the other; some people, like Gary, may be limited to only one modality; and some people may have to use all the modalities in order to learn.

USING LEARNING STYLES TO REDUCE STRESS

The Dunn and Dunn model offers many appropriate choices and allows the student to control his or her learning environment, thus reducing stress. Dunn and Dunn recognize that some individuals learn better in an informal rather than a formal environment. This model allows the teacher to say to the students: "Please find a place where you can learn." In "Introduction to Learning Styles and Brain Behavior" (1992), Dunn points out that for many students, that place is not a chair at a desk!

> When a person is seated in a hard chair, fully 75 percent of the total body weight is supported by 4 square inches of bone. The resulting stress on the tissues of the buttocks causes fatigue, discomfort, and frequent postural

change—for which many youngsters are scolded on a daily basis. Only people who, by nature, happen to be sufficiently well-padded exactly where they need to be, can tolerate conventional seating. (p. 29).

Another leading expert (Garger 1990) points out the need to allow students to engage in activities that may accompany their learning style:

> In personal classroom experience working with high school students, I found that making the perennial gum chewer throw out his gum or making a student stop her constant fidgeting (whether they were disturbing others or not) caused them to stop paying attention. They often became "restless, distracted, and irritable," some of the characteristics of those students having low CNS (Central Nervous System) arousal levels. (p. 121)

Dr. Rita Dunn suggests that practitioners:

- redesign conventional classrooms with cardboard boxes and other usable items placed perpendicular to the walls to create quiet, well-lit areas;
- create sections for controlled interaction with soft lighting;
- permit students to work in chairs, on carpeting, on bean bags, or on cushions (as long as they pay attention and perform better than they have previously);
- change the traditional environment by turning the lights off and reading in natural daylight (this helps underachievers and calms a restless class).

Creating these changes doesn't have to create chaos in your classroom. Establish rules for classroom decorum that you feel comfortable with—no feet on desks and shoes on chairs, no behavior that distracts anyone else from learning.

MATCHING LEARNING STYLES AND TEACHING STYLES

As we all know, learning is no longer the simple, clear-cut process we associate with the one-room schoolhouse. With the explosion of brain research done in the 1990s comes a plethora of information about how to learn. Initially, the new ideas regarding learning styles may be overwhelming and stress producing to the classroom teacher. The first thing any teacher should do is understand his or her own learning style strengths. The second thing to understand is that the teacher's *learning style* produces his or her own unique *teaching style*. Matching teaching styles to students' learning styles is an efficient method of increasing teacher productivity and student learning in the classroom. With increased ease in teaching and learning comes decreased stress.

In his textbook, *Curriculum Development for Education Reform* (1995), Henson shows that matching teaching and learning styles leads to higher academic achievement. He states:

> Several research studies have reported successful applications of the matching styles movement. Sixth-graders who had been matched with their learning style preferences had significantly higher reading scores than their counterparts who had not been matched with learning style preferences. Their attitudes were also better (Pizzo, 1981). High school students who were matched with teachers of similar styles had more positive attitudes (Copenhaver, 1979), and in a high school English class, students who were matched with their time-of-day preferences had less truancy (Shea, 1983). Dunn and colleagues (1984) perceive learning styles preferences as strengths teachers can use to design more effective learning experiences. Gelsert and Dunn (1991) say that "difficult material needs to be introduced through each student's strongest perceptual modality (preferred learning style) and then reinforced through supplementary modalities. (p. 337)

Sandra Rief (The Center for Applied Research in Education) agrees. In her book, *How to Reach and Teach*

ADD/ADHD Children (1993), Rief points out that respecting different learning styles can help students and teachers learn to respect other kinds of differences as well. She writes:

> We need to teach students to understand, respect, and value differences in themselves and others. We need to help students find their strengths and nurture them. We all benefit from being exposed to a variety of strategies and seeing the diversity of how we each look at the world and solve problems. It is a wonderful discovery that there are many ways to do things, not one right way. (p. 120)

As Rief says, when we use learning styles, we are not just teaching students how to be more successful in school, but how to be more successful in life.

CHAPTER 8

At-Risk Students

I think this has helped me control my temper. I have one bad temper. Thank you for relaxation.

—At-risk student

One of the most intimidating moments in my work as a physical therapist, (and this includes giving two-hour workshops that definitely unsettle my stomach) was when I had to face a group of "at-risk" high school students. My job was to convince them that using deep breathing/relaxation techniques and understanding their learning styles would make their lives better by making learning easier.

I'm sure my appearance wasn't too reassuring. I came walking into the classroom with tote bags full of "stuff" (relaxation aids) hanging off me like I was a pack horse. But I got their attention by turning out the lights and shining a rainbow light against the wall. The sell wasn't easy, but they soon became interested in what my tote bags had to offer. The stress balls and theraputty felt good to their hands. The theraband allowed them to stand up, move around the room, and "show off" their muscles.

Pretty soon, someone spotted a teddy bear's ear sticking out of a shopping bag. (I wanted my bear to stay hidden for fear I might insult them. I was only going to bring it out if all else failed.) And before I knew it, the bear was being passed around the room with a few snide comments, but with sweetness reflected in their faces. I was deep in my presentation when someone said out loud: "Look at Melvin!"

Melvin was a big, tough football player who immediately became the focus of attention. Before he could respond, all the eyes in the room could see Melvin cuddling the bear next to his cheek, with a tender expression on his face. He responded, of course, by pushing the bear away and looking embarrassed. Someone else said to their counselor, "Mrs. Roark, that was a Kodak moment!" With coaxing from the other students, Melvin graciously resumed his posture with the bear and "the Kodak moment" was preserved.

Not only did the bear help relieve Melvin's initial boredom, it also helped me stop being so nervous.

LEARNING STRESS MANAGEMENT

The "at-risk" class had a variety of struggling students. Some had AD/HD, some had behavior disorders and learning disabilities (but not severe enough to qualify for special classes), some had poor attendance, and others had no support at home.

Fig. 8–1. Melvin's "Kodak moment."

They met in small groups of three to four for thirty minutes a day for eight weeks. I taught them how to identify physical tension and how to alleviate or reduce it. I introduced them to learning styles and showed them how to use alternate classroom accommodations to increase their efficiency in learning.

It didn't take long for most of the students to warm up to the concepts. However, there's always one exception. My exception was a model-thin, blond-haired, green-eyed beauty who single-handedly made me wish that I had never started this program. Wendy had been suspended for fighting with another girl, biting her severely enough to require stitches at the emergency room. She made me wonder if the things I believed in had any relevance to high school students.

I couldn't have won her over without the help of her classmates. The other students in her group felt cheated when she used their precious time to elaborate on how "stupid this is." Wendy did, however, love to hold my $10 rainbow koosh ball. Before the beginning of relaxation time (the length of one song), the students got to pick out their "fidget": theraputty, stress balls, harmony balls, and so on. Everyone knew the rainbow koosh was off limits—nobody wanted to risk being bitten!

When the stress management classes were completed, I gave Wendy her own rainbow koosh ball. She held it, and a look of relaxed contentment replaced the hardened look she usually wore. The change in her expression was definitely worth the price of the koosh ball. This is why a tangible cue is so important. I told her I wanted her to remember the good feelings when she held the ball, whether it's a month from now or two years from now; hopefully, she'll remember and have the same sweet look on her face.

At the end of the eight-week session, Wendy made this comment on the course evaluation questionnaire: "I really enjoyed going to stress management. And I definitely have looked forward to it. Everyone should come."

USING SELF-UNDERSTANDING TO MAKE GOOD CHOICES

If "at-risk" students were taught to understand and appreciate their own learning styles and were offered classes in stress management, the knowledge would enable them to make appropriate choices when conflicts arise.

For example, if an AD/HD student is unable to settle down after recess, or from walking down a noisy hallway between classes, and if the teacher says, "Derick, you will either sit down now or go to the office," the f/f/f response kicks in and the student may not be able to make the right decision.

But by using alternate seating and classroom accommodations, the teacher can short-circuit the f/f/f response. Here's the same teacher, using a different mind set: "Derick, you can take three big breaths and go get a drink of water, or you can go sit in the rocking chair and listen to your relaxation tapes. Which do you want to do?"

There's a lot to be said for allowing students to make choices, particularly when all the choices are good. Choices that involve a combination of learning styles and stress management will give Derick a much better chance of staying in the classroom and getting back to learning.

I heard a teacher make a neat remark when I was walking past her classroom one day. She said, "I want you to find a place where you can learn." What a wonderful way to allow the student the flexibility to create his or her own learning environment, but keep the teacher totally in control. If the student is not learning, the teacher can ask the child to move: "You are not learning there."

There are so many opportunities for learning when informal classroom techniques are used. "Fidgets" can be used as tactile cues to reduce stress. The students are taught to take three deep breaths when they pick up one of these tactile cues: stress balls, kneaded erasers, thera-

Fig. 8–2. The hand and the mouth are the two most richly innervated parts of the body. Balloons filled with flour or sand provide a calming sensation to the hand and set the mood for the rest of the body.

putty, harmony balls, tube vibrators, or "thinking worms" (sport socks filled with rice). They are also told that when "your hands are happy and your body is comfortable" you will think better. Over time, these responses become automatic. We really believe that informal learning styles that include the accommodations we've talked about for managing stress, can make the difference between a student making it in school and not making it.

And we also think that good teachers, by learning to combine learning styles and stress management, will last longer and have more of themselves to give to their students and their families.

Pretty powerful statements...but in our capacities as a physical therapist and a teacher, we have seen it work. And the real reward—the feedback so many of us need but rarely get—is the difference we see in the students. Happy, busy, learning students, which makes for happy, busy, teaching teachers.

CHAPTER 9

Attention Deficit/Hyperactive Disorder Student

A good way to start this chapter about AD/HD students is with a very simple statement: "God, help me to know the difference between things I can and cannot change."

AD/HD is a biological disorder. In his book, It's *Nobody's Fault* (1996), Dr. Harold Koplewicz says that AD/HD and other neuro-biological disorders are just a matter of losing a game of DNA Russian roulette. AD/HD students have a biological problem with neurotransmitters. They can't filter out unimportant things in the environment, which means they are always on overload. They also may have sensory motor deficits, and definite—sometimes limited—learning styles.

But we can help AD/HD students compensate for their problems with the right tools. This chapter will discuss some of those tools—all of which are based on reducing stress and attending to students' learning styles.

SOURCES OF STRESS

AD/HD students have more sources of stress than other students. First, their work performance can be very inconsistent. This can be stressful for the teacher, who has seen the child succeed before and wants him or her to do so again. It is equally stressful for the AD/HD student to be told, "You just aren't trying hard enough. I've seen you do this before." Conditions have to be perfect for an AD/HD student to focus: enough sleep, no perceived threat, interesting subject matter, a comfortable work space. Asking the AD/HD child to focus well all the time is like asking a record-breaking Olympic athlete to break the record every day. You wouldn't tell the Olympic athlete, "You're just not trying hard enough. I've seen you do it before!"

For the AD/HD student, being reprimanded for lack of focus only increases the stress—and that decreases the learning. Stress makes it even more difficult than usual for the AD/HD student to filter out unimportant infor-

Fig. 9–1. Possible sensory motor deficits.

```
                        ADHD
            BIOLOGICAL PROBLEMS:
          Possible Sensory/Motor Deficits

1. Increased sensitivity   2. Poor fine      3. Poor muscle tone/postural
to sound, touch, light     motor skills      stability (can't stand to sit
                                             for long periods of time)

Becomes irritated by:     Can't keep up with   Becomes frustrated by
• certain sounds          written work         having to stay in seated
• too bright light                             position too long
• sudden touch or
• threat of sudden touch

                          STRESS!
```

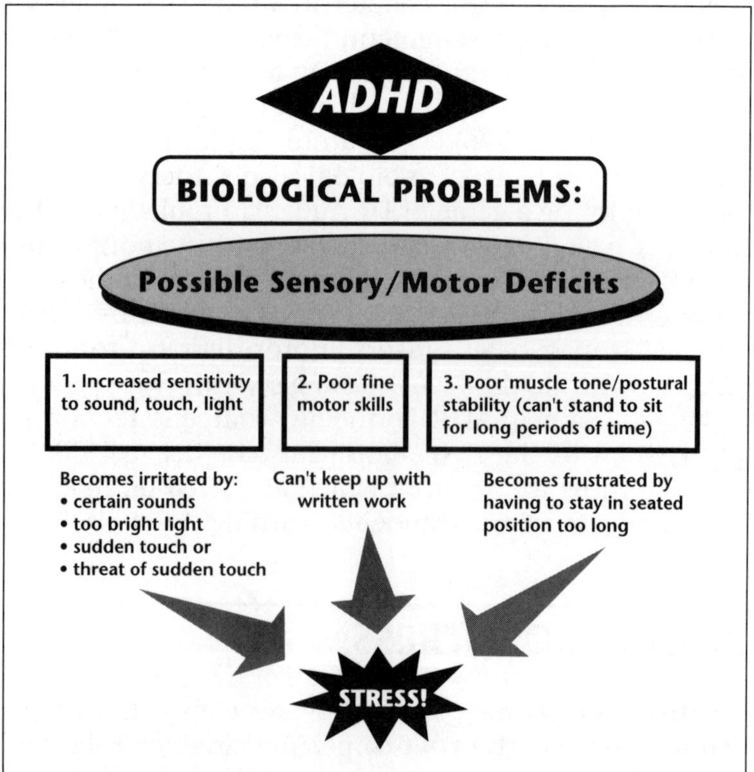

mation. In addition, the AD/HD student may also have sensory motor deficits that lead to increased sensitivity to sound, touch, and light. He or she may have poor fine and gross motor skills, as well as poor muscle tone and postural stability, which make it difficult to sit still for long periods of time. Put all these factors together, and the chances are that the AD/HD student is going to have a very hard time learning.

Another source of stress for AD/HD students is their difficulty not just *getting* to the relaxed state necessary for learning, but *staying* there. Let me give you an example. Let's say that the class is just finishing up relaxation exercises—deep breathing and stretching—and everyone is settling down nicely when…someone knocks on the door. It's a student from the office with a note for a student who's not there. It takes three seconds to tell the "messenger" that the student is absent and to write "absent" on the piece of paper.

After the messenger leaves, the relaxation time is continued. No one is upset by the knock on the door—no one, that is, but the AD/HD student, who is back to step one of the relaxation breathing and stretches. But the teacher doesn't have time to go back to step one with just one student. And that one student is now babbling on about why so-and-so is absent and maybe wants to go to the office and explain since so-and-so's mom probably forgot to call in. The rest of the class is now starting to write in their journals, but the AD/HD student is still back at the knock on the door.

You have some options to help this student re-focus. If informal seating is a choice, this might be a good time to send the student with AD/HD to the bean bag for journal writing. Or better yet, ask the student if there is a place where he or she would like to go for a few more deep breaths, and then start the journal.

You might think, "But if I let one student do it, I have to let them all." *Not true.* The teacher can say, "This is what Johnny needs to learn." Most of the students already know that anyway. So alternate seating will probably work, until someone drops a notebook, and once again, the AD/HD student's head pops back up to see what the noise was. Remember, the AD/HD student is not trying to be difficult. *He or she cannot filter out unimportant things in the environment.* Your understanding, and that of the other students in the class, is essential to the AD/HD student's ability to learn.

TAKING CONTROL

Because of their biological problem, it is crucial for AD/HD students to learn to take control of their behavior as much as possible. You can help them learn the skills to do that. Remember, little or no learning can take place when the student is under the influence of the f/f/f response. By recognizing the signs, a teacher can remind the child to "take three big breaths and relax your shoulders" so "you can think better."

There are three major techniques you can use to help the AD/HD student gain motor control, which is the first step in gaining behavioral control.

Alternate Seating: Simply allowing distracted students to sit elsewhere can help them calm down. Helpful options might include:

- a variety of different kinds of chairs—bean bag chair, rocking chair, beach chair, or video chairs;
- sitting on floor with the back supported;
- lying on a mat in a prone position, leaning on the elbows;
- standing at the desk; or
- whatever works!

Classroom Accommodations: As earlier chapters describe, simple accommodations can help an AD/HD student take control and focus on learning. Some options include:

- using "fidgets" (stress balls, theraputty, theraband, kneaded erasers);

Fig. 9–2. "Thinking worms" provide neutral warmth for the neck and shoulders. Their weight (two pounds of rice) facilitates the passive stretching of neck and shoulder musculature to produce a relaxation response.

- "thinking worms";
- sports bottles; and
- a headset with tapes.

Opportunities for Movement: Sometimes just using up that "need to move" helps the hyperactive child to focus. Have the student:

- take notes to the office.
- take heavy boxes to the office that will later be returned to the classroom, possibly by another hyperactive student during another hour.
- take trips to the drinking fountain, chalkboard, or exercise bike.

In today's fitness-oriented world, an exercise bicycle, rowing machine, or stepper in your classroom would not be out of place. Using this equipment could be a reward for completed work for any student, and could provide an outlet for the hyperactive child. And here's a bonus: the teacher can use the equipment too. A few minutes taken from a conference hour to get rid of stress is time well spent.

Our high school has a treadmill in the teachers' lounge. Smart, smart, smart! There are regulars who use it, but I've also noticed that some of the teachers who used to walk by and grin at me walking the devil out of that thing are using it if they are having a bad day.

The thing about exercise, both for students and teachers, is that if you "walk that thing" regularly, you won't have as many bad days. Or let me rephrase that. You may have as many bad days, but you'll be able to handle them better if you've walked or rowed or stepped the bad stuff out of your system.

These methods—alternate seating, classroom accommodations, and opportunities for movement—are simple ways to teach a child to stop the effects of the f/f/f response and to control movement when the brain does not inhibit it automatically. Research indicates that stress increases when people feel that they have no control over a situation. Using these techniques in your classroom can help give these students a feeling of control over their bodies, and that, in itself, reduces stress.

I cannot emphasize these methods enough. Many AD/HD children have no idea that they have a great deal of control over themselves. They feel that they are riding a runaway horse and can do nothing but hold on for dear life. They have never considered just taking three big breaths and saying "Whoa horse!" Once children have learned how to prevent the effects of the f/f/f response and how to channel their excess need to move toward purposeful activity, they have tools they can always draw on to reduce stress and increase learning.

CHAPTER 10

Hidden Disorders

I attended a sensory integration conference once, where the frustrated mother of an AD/HD student with sensory motor deficits said: "It would be easier if my son were in a wheelchair—at least then people would know how disabled he really is." Yes, I thought. That is so true for all of us, whether we're parents, teachers, or therapists. It is hard to believe any disorder is present when the child appears to be perfectly "normal."

We need to understand that even mild sensory motor deficits can affect lives in a major way. That's why it's important to discuss hidden disorders, which are usually familiar only to physical and occupational therapists. When we learn to recognize these disorders, we can provide accommodations that will make learning possible, as we do with "at-risk" or AD/HD students. These children, even more than others, may need alternate seating, "fidgets" to occupy their hands, and opportunities for frequent movement.

LOW MUSCLE TONE

Muscle tone refers to the degree of tension in the muscles of the body when they are at rest. This can be thought of as a muscle's "readiness" to perform movement. Normal tone has been described as the state of muscle tone that is high enough to permit movement against gravity, yet low enough to allow complete freedom of movement.

Deviations in muscle tone range from severely reduced muscle tone (hypotonia or low muscle tone), to an excess of muscle tone (hypertonia or spasticity).

Children with low muscle tone tend to rest their head on the desk. It takes entirely too much effort to hold the head up, so they either prop it up with one hand or lay it on the desk. These children cannot sit at their desks. They generally half sit, half stand, with the upper part of the body "draped" over the desk. They like to put both feet in the seat of the chair or tip the chair backwards. They have a very loose grip and can barely hold onto a pencil.

Use this exercise to check for extremely low muscle tone. (Mild deficits won't show up this way.) Hold your hand out with the palm up—fingers should be relaxed but curled up slightly.

Ask your students, "Can everyone hold your hand like mine?" This is the easiest way to see what muscle tone is. See how your fingers are curled and ready to go to work, even though your hands are resting? If a child with low muscle tone were asked to put his or her hand in this position, it might lay flat without any curling up of his fingers. When a muscle has low tone, it takes a lot of energy to get the muscle in a position to go to work. Think of holding a pencil. The same is true for sitting. Holding the body upright against gravity is a monumental job for a person who has low muscle tone in the muscles of the back and chest.

People with low muscle tone have what physical and occupational therapists call poor postural stability or postural fatigue. That means they get so tired of sitting they

Fig. 10–1. The simple act of moving from one seating area to another allows the muscles of the student with low muscle tone to become rested and ready to work again.

can't think. In an informal learning style setting, people with low muscle tone can change positions often. Each sitting position requires slightly different muscles to do the major work. Alternate seating—bean bag chairs, rocking chairs, video chairs, ball chairs, exercise mats with back supported against the wall, or lying prone on elbows or standing at a desk—can make a world of difference to students with low muscle tone. (They can use clip boards, masonite squares, or lap desks for written work in these positions.) In addition to allowing them to change seating regularly, give them frequent movement breaks (walking to the pencil sharpener, chalkboard, drinking fountain, or office.) The very act of moving helps stimulate the muscle tone and allows fatigued muscles to get rest.

As one expert in the field sums up the benefit of an informal learning style for children with muscle tone disorder, "When students are not forced to work against their bodies' natural preferences, they feel more relaxed at school and accepted, and the end result is often better learning." (Garger 1990)

SENSORY MOTOR DEFICITS

Sensory motor development allows us to relate to our world in an easy, meaningful, and automatic manner through the following sensory systems: tactile, vestibular (balance), proprioceptive (awareness of the body in space), olfactory (smell), gustatory (taste), visual, and auditory.

Students with sensory motor deficits are the ones who:

- are always standing on your feet or somebody else's.
- have such poor body awareness, they are always bumping into someone or something.
- generally walk down the hall with a hand running along the wall to keep track of where they are. If their hands aren't on the wall, they are on someone or carrying something.
- always have something in their mouths.
- either overreact or underreact to a situation.
- may cry over the slightest scrape or ignore a stream of blood running down their leg.
- may be ready to fight someone who touches their back but continually wants to hug others.
- may complain that the lights are too bright or the noise too loud.

Failure of the sensory motor system to develop fully causes a child to demonstrate difficulty with:

- body awareness.
- sorting or screening out irrelevant stimuli.
- feeling secure while moving in space.
- using two sides of the body together.
- planning a new motor task.

When these mechanisms or tools are not automatic, the child is forced to "think through" these tasks using the higher-level learning centers in the brain that ideally should be reserved for conceptual learning. Children with sensory motor deficits frequently demonstrate "acting out" behaviors due to frustration with their inability to perform simple motor tasks that others can do automatically.

An informal learning style classroom allows these children to "self-regulate" by having classroom accommodations available. These accommodations—hearing protectors, headsets/relaxation tapes, "white noise" tapes, "thinking worms"—help the child filter out unimportant or irritating stimuli.

Sam's Story

I can't talk about low muscle tone and sensory deficits without telling you about Sam. I was asked to do a physical therapy evaluation on Sam when he was in the first grade. I was told that in addition to AD/HD, Sam had a bad attitude and often exploded in the classroom, being disrespectful to the teacher.

I picked Sam up at his classroom and after introductions, I reached for his hand to begin walking downstairs to our testing area. Sam's hand was limp—it felt like a glove filled with some kind of inanimate stuffing—and he did not hold my hand back. He barely lifted his feet from the ground and ended each step with a thud. When we reached the stairs, he propped his forearms on the rail, pressed his shoulder to the wall and stepping on his own feet occasionally, proceeded down the steps. When coming up the stairs, he pulled himself up with the help of the railing.

Sam, a straight A student, had extremely low muscle tone (hypotonia) plus sensory motor deficits. Sam did not know where his body was much of the time. He had no concept of personal space (his own or mine) and frequently stepped on my feet. His mother said that she had seen him literally fall down three times before he finished brushing his teeth at the bathroom sink.

Despite all this, Sam had a wonderful third grade year. (Not that there weren't a few ups and downs.) His teacher, Mrs. Glascock, had an informal teaching style. The alternate seating and classroom accommodations that Sam needed for survival fit right into the loose structure Mrs. Glascock already employed.

Fig. 10–2. Alternate seating (bean bag chair) and classroom accommodations (headset with white noise tape or classical music) helped Sam succeed in the classroom.

Sam also had some sensory defensive behaviors: he withdrew from sudden and unexpected touch, was overly sensitive to sound and light, and had postural insecurity. The "cost of living," both physically and motionally, was enormous for Sam. Everything Sam did during the day—from putting his clothes on to sitting in his seat to writing down his math problems—required more energy than it should have. It's no wonder he needed extra tools for decreasing his stress.

SENSORY DEFENSIVENESS

A tendency to react negatively or with alarm to sensory input that is generally considered harmless or non-irritating is typical of sensory defensiveness. Common symptoms may include over-sensitivity to light or unexpected touch and sudden movement or overreaction to unstable surfaces, high frequency noises, excesses of noise or visual stimuli, and certain smells.

Sensory defensiveness results in varying degrees of stress and anxiety, although symptoms vary with each individual. The child with sensory defensiveness may misperceive the world as dangerous, alarming, or at the very least irritating. Learned patterns and habits are often developed around avoiding disrupting sensory events or seeking out sensation that might restore comfort. Innocent memories can be stored as traumatic experiences. Relationships can be exaggerated. Behavior with known and trusted people can be quite different than with others. These behaviors make sense if one realizes that the child is doing the best he or she can to "survive."

Levels Of Severity

In their ground-breaking book, *Sensory Defensiveness in Children Aged 2–12*, Wilbarger and Wilbarger have identified sensory defensiveness as level I (mild), level II (moderate) and level III (severe).

- **Level I-Mild:** While appearing quite "normal," children with mild defensiveness might be described as picky, over-sensitive, slightly overactive, resistive to change, or slightly controlling. They can act mildly irritated by some sensations, but not by others. They may be picky about clothes or food. While these children can achieve at age level in school or have good social relations, they may have to use enormous control and effort to succeed in these areas. When they can no longer maintain the level of effort to do so, they may "fall apart" emotionally under apparently little or no stress.

- **Level II-Moderate:** Moderate sensory defensiveness affects two or more aspects of a child's life. At this level, children often have difficulty with social relations, either being overly aggressive or isolating themselves from peers. Many self-care skills are disrupted, such as dressing, bathing, and eating. Children may have difficulty with attention or behavior in school. Exploration and play may be limited due to fearfulness of new situations and resistance to change.

- **Level III-Severe:** A severe sensory defensiveness disrupts every aspect of a child's life. These children usually have other diagnostic labels for various areas of dysfunction (e.g., severe developmental delay, autism, autistic-like behavior, or emotionally disturbed). Strong avoidance of some kinds of sensations—or the reverse, intense sensory seeking—are common. Sensory defensiveness may block development and/or interfere with treatment of these children. Treating sensory defensiveness first reduces sensory problems and increases the effectiveness of other forms of intervention.

From *Sensory Defensiveness in Children Aged 2–12*, © 1991, Wilbarger P. and Wilbarger J. L., Reprinted with permission.

OPTIMUM LEVELS OF AROUSAL

Our attention, alertness, and perception depend upon having optimum levels of arousal.

When a child has sensory defensiveness, major and minor sensory events create changeable levels of stress and anxiety. Intervention is possible when we understand how certain kinds of events either disrupt the child or contribute to his or her recovery from disturbing events. The following chart shows four types of individuals all responding to small irritations or large disturbances. Notice that the individual without sensory defensiveness recovers from these events while other types of individuals never return to the optimal level of arousal.

From *Sensory Defensiveness in Children Aged 2–12*, © 1991, Wilbarger, P. and Wilbarger, J.L. Reprinted with permission.

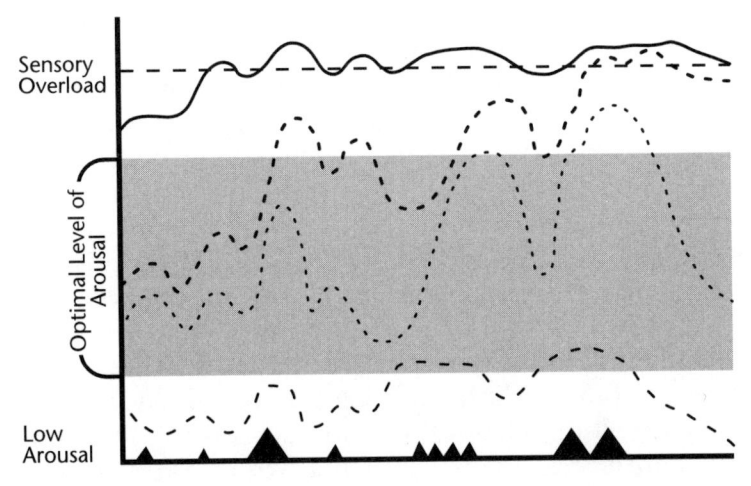

This chart shows typical patterns of change in arousal in response to environmental events. Four types of children are responding to small irritations (▲) or large disturbances (▲).

KEY	
——— Child who experiences overload, or sensory shut-down.	- - - Sensory defensive child.
····· Child with a nondefensive system.	_ _ _ Child who is under responsive or has sensory registration problems

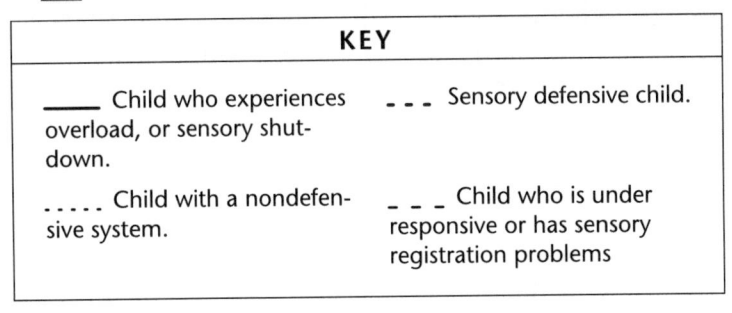

Fig. 10–3. Optimum Levels of Arousal

Perhaps it is not surprising that many of the students in the behavior disordered classroom have sensory defensive behaviors, and I was able to help these students relax—and learn. I began taking the boys in small groups (two or three at a time) and introducing them to the concepts of "three big breaths," "loose as a goose," and "stiff as a board." While those first years had their rocky moments, I quickly figured out that the more relaxation toys I had to show the boys, the more interested they became.

One of the highlights of my "accidental discovery" came the day one of the boys marched in, gave a big whoosh of relief and said : "Aunt Janet, I thought you'd never get here. I been needin' this!" And he promptly grabbed the weighted bear (with the heart that beat slowly and steadily inside his jacket), flopped down on the mat, clutched the bear to his chest, and began to get calm. He sighed happily and grinned up at me.

My bag of tricks grew! Teachers began calling me "the bag lady"—and I could barely drag the bag by this time! Things like the rocking board and the relaxation barrel could stay at school, but now my repertoire consisted of soft lighting via battery-powered lanterns, windmills for blowing, pretty music, eye pillows, hand-held massagers to "loosen" muscles—all this in addition to my standby theraputty, stress balls, "thinking worms," and weighted bears.

Once the students relaxed, they wanted more. They realized that they were in control and had choices to make about what "things" it took to help them relax. They each made a list of "things that help me relax" and were able to identify their favorites. These tangible cues were theirs to take back to their classrooms. More important, the students had gained control with their new ability to calm themselves.

I discovered that most students in the behavior disordered classroom have very poor body awareness. They could not identify "right" or "left" body parts. When I asked them to lie on their backs, they'd lie on their tummies. They literally didn't know their backs from their fronts. Many were unable to close their eyes voluntarily, blow their noses, or blow out through their mouths, indicating poor oral/facial awareness. They had no concept of "personal space" and were constantly in other people's space. Many displayed characteristics of children who had sensory problems: they either overreacted or underreacted to pain, sound, light, or touch. They also had poor posture while sitting and standing, which indicated low muscle tone.

So it appeared to me that many of their behaviors had a *physical origin*. As I got to know the class better, it was obvious that most of them had learning problems. Most had a diagnosis of learning disabilities and a few were EMH. Nearly all had a diagnosis of AD/HD. I have come to believe that these children were not truly "behavior disordered," but rather that their behavior was a result of being unable to deal with the stress of having many physical and learning problems.

Warren's Story

One day I walked into the behavior disordered room and witnessed a stand-off between the teacher's aide and Warren. "Warren won't take his spelling test," the aide explained. After some coaxing, I convinced Warren to take three big breaths "so you can spell better." Warren's tantrums were as famous as his inability to spell. I proceeded to round up my next students and leave the room (and said a little prayer for good spelling results.) When I returned to the room thirty minutes later, Warren and the aide were beaming. Warren said, "I made a 100% on my test!" This was a first for Warren. He may have thought, "If I can calm myself, I can spell those words too!"

PROVIDING ACCOMMODATIONS

I had a classroom experience ten years ago that illustrates how teachers can provide accommodations for students, even when they don't know the exact cause of students' learning problems.

I looked up from my desk, thinking about an upcoming test one of my ninth grade students was going to be taking, and what I saw hit me hard. My learning disordered classroom used to be a large art supply closet.

What I saw in this very small space made me want to laugh out loud.

Dennis, a rather large boy, was lying on the floor writing, because the desk was too small for him and because he could write better lying down than he could sitting up. Matt, who preferred to move his desk to the corner and lean against the wall, then scrunch down eye level with his paper and write sideways, was also busy writing. That left Bert in the other corner, sitting in his desk with a wet paper towel over his head because he got so hot and could work better when he was cooler—plus he had less distractions when he was under the towel.

What a group this fifth hour was! I thought. Each working so hard, each doing his own thing, each....

"Mrs. Nunn?"

I looked up. It was the principal.

"Yes?"

"We have several visitors here I'd like...several...." He stopped dead. He had looked past me into the classroom.

My students accuse me of having an uncontrollable laugh, which to me just means loud. But at this particular moment, I felt if I did laugh it would indeed be uncontrollable.

"Yes, yes," I heard myself say. "Come in...or, that is...." He couldn't come in. There wasn't any room. Dennis was lying in front of my desk. "Er...stick your head in and look around." I saw two other heads look past the principal's head. The two other men's eyes also seemed to pop.

Dennis looked up from the floor and said, "Hi."

Matt, scrunched down eye-level with his desk and four feet of legs and feet stuck out in front of him, nodded and went on writing.

But it was Bert under the paper towel who about did me in. The towel whooshed in and out when he talked and he asked, "Who is it?"

I couldn't help it. Some of my suppressed laughter escaped, sounding a little like a bark. I tried to pretend I was clearing my throat. "It's Dr. Whitmore and several visitors," I managed, very pleased that my voice quavered only slightly. I waited a second, hoping Bert would remember what I'd told him to do if anyone ever came in unexpectedly. My pause was rewarded.

He lifted the front of the paper towel and greeted the guests politely. "It gets hot in here," he added as an afterthought. Then he dropped the towel back down and continued to write. I was very proud of him.

Our visitors, by this time, were beginning to back out the door. Probably for two reasons: Bert wasn't lying. Even though we had a fan on, it was hot in here. We were next to an art room with a kiln backed up against the side wall to our left. The other reason was the visitors were speechless. What could they say about such an outlandish-looking situation?

And we heard one of the men ask the principal as they walked away, "What kind of classroom was that?"

I giggled and shook my head.

The students looked up, even Bert from under his towel, and smiled back. We had made progress! A few months ago I would have been upset at such a remark, especially if the students had heard it. And they would have been more upset. Now we looked at each other and knew. This was a classroom where students had learning disabilities and we simply learned to work around them—to compensate. And here was the "biggie." (Although it's only been in the last few years that I've learned this.) There were reasons—good neurological reasons—why Bert could do better work from under his paper towel, and why Dennis could write better lying on the floor (aside from the fact that his desk was too small.), and why Matt was writing with his head even with the paper and eyeing his words slantwise.

"What kind of classroom was that?" Dennis mimicked and snorted from the floor. "That man's ignert."

I chuckled. "Yep."

There were other grunts of agreement. Bert muttered from under his towel, "He don't know nothin' bout learnin' different." The towel whooshed in and out.

Again, I restrained the urge to laugh aloud, knowing what we must have looked like to the visiting administrators.

Ten years later, I know that these students had poor muscle tone, and they were finding their own learning styles to compensate.

And I'm thankful that the students knew what accomodations they needed to work and learn. Because about all I knew at the time was that if I let them do what they needed to do, they succeeded.

CHAPTER 11

Re-framing Mind-Set

The most important stress reliever for teachers and students is the teacher's *mind-set*. How does the teacher make sense of something? How does he or she define it? When teachers understand that the cause of AD/HD is an imbalance of neurochemicals, they know that the student is just trying to survive. If, on the other hand, a teacher's mind-set says, "This kid is out to get me," both teacher *and* student lose. We believe that the teacher's mind-set affects everything in the classroom. It can make or break a teacher, and it can make or break a child.

Re-framing mind-set is just another way of saying—Look at it in a different way, or use a new frame of reference. Richard Bandler and John Grinder, founders of Neuro-linguistic Programming, a powerful scientific method that helps people re-frame meanings, tell the story of a woman who was driving her family crazy by being obsessively neat. She vacuumed the rug constantly and became enormously upset if anyone walked on it. Bandler and Grinder first helped the woman into a relaxed state—that is, they elicited the *relaxation response*—where mental connections would be more flexible and new associations could be made. Then they had the woman imagine what her house would be like if there were no one there to mess up the rug. No husband to love, no children to delight her. Just a clean rug. She began to associate a perfect rug with being lonely, and a *new frame of reference* was born. Once she began to see the situation from this vantage point, she delighted in imagining her loved ones returning and walking over her precious rug! (Borysenko, 1987)

As educators, we can do important re-framing around stress management and learning styles. We really believe that teachers can do themselves and their students a lifetime service by taking a few minutes before each class to relax with deep breathing and stretching, and by not being afraid to pursue different learning styles for certain students.

What we are beginning to discover about the role of emotions and stress in learning challenges basic assumptions about traditional education. Putting this information to use in the classroom requires a major shift in our mind-set. Just as the woman in the example above had to change the *meaning* she associated with the clean rug, we need to consider the possibility that traditional testing, grading, and classroom structure may not always benefit the teacher or the student.

CREATING AN ATMOSPHERE FOR LEARNING

As Caine and Caine point out in *Understanding a Brain-Based Approach to Learning and Teaching* (1992), those of us who work in schools must recognize that learning happens most readily when learners are relaxed. It is up to teachers, then, to create an atmosphere that makes learning possible. In addition, teachers must learn to relax themselves if they are to help their students. As Caine and Caine put it:

> The subtle signals that emanate from a teacher also have an impact on learning. Our inner states show in skin color, muscular tension and posture, rate of breathing, eye movements and so on. Teachers should engage the

interests and enthusiasm of students through their own enthusiasm, coaching and modeling, so that the unconscious signals relating to the importance and value of what is being learned are appropriate.

It is important to practice what we preach and to express genuine feelings rather than to fake them, because our true inner states are always signaled and discerned at some level by learners. (p. 125)

In terms of re-framing mind-set, it's a good idea for teachers to remember that maintaining a relaxed atmosphere in the classroom won't *prevent* you from meeting curriculum deadlines, it will actually *help you get there!*

I took a course several summers ago from a wonderful teacher with a great sense of humor, Dr. Dick English, who said: "I can guarantee some of you will walk away from this class and remember very little about what you've worked so hard to learn, but you will always remember my stories." And he was right. So we'll end this chapter with three stories about how we learned to re-frame mind-set.

The "Spitter"

I learned the importance of mind-set in my first job as a physical therapist. "The Spitter" taught me.

I was working at the Rusk Rehabilitation Center in Columbia, Missouri. I considered "people skills" my strong suit and thought I could get along with anybody. However, one of my first patients was an 80-pound, 80-year-old woman who had had a stroke and needed some painful exercises to her shoulder and hand. No matter what I did or how hard I tried, the little lady would scream at me, yelling "Stop it!" at the top of her lungs, spitting at me in what I came to believe was sort of an exclamation point summing up how she felt about me.

I was embarrassed to think about the intense feelings of dislike I had for this helpless little woman. But I eventually realized that her reactions towards me were not personal. I re-framed my thinking. She had suffered trauma to the brain and was striking out at everyone who "threatened" her.

I began having her take three big breaths while playing soothing music when she came for her physical therapy. This broke the f/f/f cycle and allowed her to stop feeling threatened every time she saw me. This small window of time allowed me to do her exercises without making her agitated. She even began calling me "dear!"

Shannon's Story

A teacher who re-frames a volatile situation into one that can be resolved calmly, automatically decreases the "threat" a child may be feeling, lessens stress, and keeps the disruption from getting in the way of learning. As long as the teacher does not perceive the situation to be threatening to her, the student will begin "shifting gears" and will understand that the situation is not threatening to him either.

One day Shannon, one of my ninth grade students, came in very upset at the beginning of the hour. I saw he was about to trip over the feet of one of the other students who was already seated. So I put my hand on Shannon's shoulder to guide him around the feet and said his name at the same time.

Something seemed to actually explode inside him and he "got in my face," as the students say, and proceeded to tell me never to touch him or try to push him around again. My first thought was to say, "To the office, young man!" But Shannon's reaction to me was so out of character for him that I didn't react immediately. He could get extremely agitated and he mumbled a lot, but he'd never really gotten hostile.

Two of my "football-player" sized students did react immediately, however. They had Shannon's arms pinned and were now "in his face."

"Sit down, all of you," I said more calmly than I felt.

"Mrs. Nunn, he was yelling at you. He got in your face and you won't even let us say 'shut up' to each other!"

Leo was clearly more upset with me than with Shannon by this time.

Shannon screamed, "Well then ring the buzzer for the principal and have me hauled off!"

The rest of the class nodded, seeming to agree with Shannon, and then they waited for me to do just that.

"I'll decide when I need to ring the buzzer." I worked at keeping my voice low and quiet. "Sit down, Shannon. And when you've taken some deep breaths and gotten yourself under control, come up and tell me what happened to send you in here in such a state. You are clearly not yourself."

After about five minutes, he did just that. A student in the hall had shoved him and called him a derogatory name, and a similar situation had just happened in Physical Education class. Shannon, without my urging him to do so, apologized to me and the class.

"So what are you gonna do to him if he comes in here and does it again tomorrow?" Leo was still not satisfied with my decision to let Shannon off the hook.

"I shall call on you, Leo, to pin him against the blackboard while I go buzz the buzzer." We all laughed and Shannon, for the rest of the year, was never again as agitated as he'd been during that class. And I don't think I need to say he never "got in my face" again.

I was glad, when it was over, that my "old mind-set" of teacher-sending-rowdy-student-to-office hadn't kicked in.

Jarrod's Story

My discovery of the use of deep breathing/relaxation techniques with behavior disordered children was strictly accidental. It was a matter of survival. It was also the first time I experienced the value of a change in my mind-set. One of my more difficult students was a kindergartner with cerebral palsy. He was having a hard time adjusting to school and had been kicked off the bus the first week of school. When I heard this, I said to myself, "How bad could a little kindergartner be?" I knew I'd be able to handle him.

My first treatment session was a disaster, and I ended up sitting him out in the hall for a "time out." I had never had to give a "time out" to a student before because I had a bag of tricks that no child had ever been able to refuse. Colorful koosh balls, magic wands, glow in the dark balls, and peppy music had always worked to entice a student to do the exercises I wanted him to do. But not Jarrod! After several weeks of having Jarrod sit in the hallway during his treatment time, I decided that "something's gotta change" because it wasn't going to be Jarrod.

One day I went to pick Jarrod up in his classroom and he was in "time out" with a red, splotched face from crying. He had been refusing to do his work again. I truly felt sorry for him and at that moment no longer saw him as a threat to getting my job done. On our way to the physical therapy room, I said: "You know what, Jarrod, you just need to come get on the rocking board and relax."

That was the turning point in our relationship. My mind-set changed from getting him to do what I wanted him to do, to doing what he needed. My mind-set was

Fig. 11–1. The vibration from the music of a small tape recorder placed on this student's chest adds to the calming sensation of the rocking board.

re-framed. After that day, he always knew his relaxation time came first. After five minutes of relaxation, he never refused the other things I wanted him to do.

RE-FRAMING THE AD/HD STUDENT

Reducing teacher stress regarding AD/HD students still goes back to those simple words: re-framing mind-set. You will be able to re-frame mind-set if you remember that an AD/HD student's lack of success in the classroom is biological in origin...not motivational.

We need to look at classroom behavior for the AD/HD child in a different way. Doesn't a picture look totally different when a new picture frame is placed around it? Teachers who understand that AD/HD children are "just trying to survive" experience less stress than teachers who think that the AD/HD student is "just trying to make my life miserable." The most important stress reliever for teachers and the student is the mind-set of the teacher. As long as teachers understand the power of the f/f/f response, they will not fall into the trap of thinking that this student is doing this to *me*.

So, take three big breaths, stretch, and relax. Congratulations! You've just finished a book you may have been too stressed out to read when you started!

Bibliography

BOOKS:

Ayres, A. J. 1979. *Sensory Integration and the Child.* Los Angeles: Western Psychological Services.

Barkley, R. A. 1990. *Attention-Deficit Hyperactivity Disorder: A Handbook for Diagnosis and Treatment.* New York: Guilford Press.

Benson, H. 1975. *The Relaxation Response.* New York: Morrow.

Bloom, F. E., and Lazerson, A. 1988. *Brain, Mind, and Behavior.* New York: W. H. Freeman.

Borysenko, J. 1987. *Minding the Body, Mending the Mind.* Reading, Mass.: Addison-Wesley.

Brazelton, T. B. 1992. *Touchpoints: Your Child's Emotional and Behavioral Development.* Reading, Mass.: Addison-Wesley.

Burr, L. A., ed. 1986. *Therapy Through Movement: Integrating the Physical and Psychological Self.* Nottingham: Nottingham Rehab Limited.

Caine, R. N., and Caine, G. 1992. "Understanding a Brain-Based Approach to Learning and Teaching." In *A Review of Articles and Books.* Edited by R. Dunn. New York: School of Education and Human Services, St. John's University.

Chopra, D. 1990. *Quantum Healing: Exploring the Frontiers of Mind/Body Medicine*. New York: Bantam Books.

Damasio, A. R. 1994. *Descartes' Error: Emotion, Reason, and the Human Brain*. New York: G. P. Putnam.

Davis, M., Eshelman, E. R., and McKay, M. 1995. *The Relaxation and Stress Reduction Workbook*. Oakland, Calif.: New Harbinger Publications.

de Quirâos, J. B., and Schrager, O. L. 1979. *Neuropsychological Fundamentals in Learning Disabilities*. Novato, Calif.: Academic Therapy Publications.

Dunn, R. 1992. "Introduction to Learning Styles and Brain Behavior." In *A Review of Articles and Books*. Edited by R. Dunn. New York: School of Education and Human Services, St. John's University.

———1992. "Redesigning the Conventional Classroom To Respond to Learning Style Differences." In *A Review of Articles and Books*. Edited by R. Dunn. New York: School of Education and Human Services, St. John's University.

Dunn, R., Beaudry J. S., and Clavas A. 1989. "Survey of Research on Learning Styles." In *A Review of Articles and Books, Part 2*. Edited by R. Dunn. New York: School of Education and Human Services, St. John's University.

Dychtwald, K. 1977. *Bodymind*. New York: Pantheon Books.

Everett, T., Dennis, M., and Ricketts, E., eds. 1995. *Physiotherapy in Mental Health: A Practical Approach*. Oxford: Butterworth-Heinemann

Garger, S. 1992. "Is There A Link Between Learning Style and Neurophysiology?" In *A Review of Articles and Books*. Edited by R. Dunn. New York: School of Education and Human Services, St. John's University.

Goleman, D. 1995. *Emotional Intelligence*. New York: Bantam Books.

Gutloff, K., ed. 1996. *Multiple Intelligences*. Washington, D. C.: National Education Association

Henson, K. T. 1995. *Curriculum Development for Education Reform*. New York: HarperCollins College Publishers.

Howard, P. J. 1994. *The Owner's Manual for The Brain: Everyday Applications from Mind-Brain Research*. Austin, Texas: Leornian Press.

Hynd, G. W., and Obrzut, J. E., eds. 1981. *Neuropsychological Assessment and the School-Age Child: Issues and Procedures*. New York: Grune & Stratton.

Kabat-Zinn, J. 1994. *Wherever You Go, There You Are: Mindfulness Meditation in Everyday Life*. New York: Hyperion.

Koplewicz, H. S. 1996. *It's Nobody's Fault: New Hope for Difficult Children and Their Parents*. New York: Random House.

Lara, A. 1994. *Slowing Down in a Speeded-Up World*. Berkeley, Calif.: Conari Press.

Lehr, J. B., and Harris, H. W. 1988. *At-Risk, Low-Achieving Students in the Classroom*. Washington, D. C.: National Education Association

Levine, B. H. *Your Body Believes Every Word You Say*. Boulder Creek, Calif.: Aslan Publishing.

Littell, E. H. 1990. *Basic Neuroscience for the Health Professions*. Thorofare, N. J.: Slack, Inc.

Matlin, M. W. 1988. *Sensation and Perception*. Boston: Allyn and Bacon

Merrill, S. C., ed. 1990. *Environment: Implications for Occupational Therapy Practice: A Sensory Integrative Perspective*. Rockville, Md.: American Occupational Therapy Association.

Moser, A. 1988. *Don't Pop Your Cork On Mondays!: The Children's Anti-Stress Book*. Kansas City: Landmark Editions.

Moyers, B. 1993. *Healing and the Mind*. New York: Doubleday.

Nelson, D. N. 1992. *Stress Management: Does Anyone in Chicago Know About It?*. Aurora, Colo.: National Writers Press.

Quinn, P. O., and Stern, J. M. 1991. *Putting on the Brakes: Young People's Guide To Understanding Attention Deficit Hyperactivity Disorder*. New York: Magination Press.

Restak, R. 1984. *The Brain*. New York: Bantam Books.

———1991. *The Brain Has a Mind of Its Own*. New York: Harmony Books.

Rief, S. F. 1993. *How To Reach and Teach ADD/ADHD Children: Practical Techniques, Strategies, and Interventions for Helping Children with Attention Problems and Hyperactivity*. West Nyack, N.Y.: The Center for Applied Research in Education.

Schwartz, T. 1995. *What Really Matters: Searching for Wisdom in America*. New York: Bantam Books.

Sheehan, D. V. 1983. *The Anxiety Disease*. New York: Scribner.

Shellenberger, S., and Williams, S. M. 1994. *How Does Your Engine Run? The Leader's Guide to the Alert Program for Self-Regulation*. Alberquerque, N. M.: Therapy Works

Silvernail, D. L. 1986. *Teaching Styles as Related to Student Achievement*. 2d ed. Washington, D. C.: National Education Association

Slap-Shelton, L., and Shapiro, L. E. 1992. *Take a Deep Breath: The Kid's Play-Away Stress Book*. King of Prussia, Penn.: The Center of Applied Psychology.

Sommer, B. L. 1993. *Psycho-Cybernetics 2000*. Englewood Cliffs, N. J.: Prentice Hall.

Steinem, G. 1992. *Revolution from Within: A Book of Self-Esteem*. Boston: Little, Brown and Company.

Swick, K. J. 1987. *Student Stress: A Classroom Management System*. Washington D. C.: National Education Association

Time-Life Editors. 1994. *Emotions: Journey Through Mind and Body*. Alexandria, Va.: Time Life Books.

Vail, P. L. 1987. *Smart Kids with School Problems: Things To Know and Ways To Help*. New York: Dutton.

Vitale, B. M. 1982. *Unicorns Are Real: A Right-Brained Approach to Learning*. Rolling Hills Estates, Calif.: Jalmar Press

———1986. *Free Flight: Celebrating Your Right Brain*. Rolling Hills Estates, Calif.: Jalmar Press.

Weiss, L. 1992. *Attention Deficit Disorder in Adults*. Dallas, Texas: Taylor Publishing

Wilbarger, P., and Wilbarger, J. L. 1991. *Sensory Defensiveness in Children Aged 2-12: An Intervention Guide for Parents and Other Caretakers*. Santa Barbara, Calif.: Avanti Educational Programs.

ARTICLES:

Anderson, E., and Emmons, B. 1996. "Sensory Integration: The Hidden Disorder." *LDA Newsbriefs* 31, no. 1 (January/February): 3–5.

Ballinger, J. 1980. "Teaching Relaxation Techniques to the Handicapped Child." Booklet, University of Missouri.

Begley, S. 1996. "Your Child's Brain." *Newsweek*, 19 February, 55–58.

Coffey, N. 1992. "Hungarian PT Unites Psychology and Therapy In Movement-Based Treatment." *P. T. Bulletin* 7, no. 19 (13 May): 32–34.

Hancock, L. N. 1996. "Why Do Schools Flunk Biology?" *Newsweek*, 19 February, 58–61.

Risko, A. 1992. "Balint Group With Physiotherapists Working With Cancer Patients." Dept. of Psychooncology, National Institute of Oncology, Budapest. Abstract presented at ESPO Congress in Beune, France.

———1986. "Body Centered Nonverbal Psychotherapy, Complex Movement Therapy." *Hungarian Psychological Review* (June): 467–497.

Wright, R. 1995. "The Evolution of Despair." *Time*, 28 August, 50–57.

TAPES:

Chopra, D. 1990. *Magical Mind, Magical Body*. Niles, Ill.: Nightingale Conant Corporation. (audio)

———1991. *Insomnia: The Complete Mind/Body Solution*. Niles, Ill.: Nightingale Conant Corporation. (audio)

———1991. *The Higher Self*. Niles, Ill.: Nightingale Conant Corporation. (audio)

———1993. *Ageless Body, Timeless Mind*. Niles, Ill.: Nightingale Conant Corporation. (audio)

Coulter, D. J. 1988. *Classroom Clues to Thinking Problems*. Longmont, Colo.: Coulter Publications. (audio)

Covey, S. 1993. *Living the Seven Habits*. Provo, Utah: Covey Leadership Center. (audio)

Metcalf, C. W. 1994. *Lighten Up!* Niles, Ill.: Nightingale Conant Corporation. (audio)

Faulkner, C., Gerling K., and Schmidt G. 1991. *NLP: The New Technology Of Achievement*. Niles, Ill.: Nightingale Conant Corporation. (audio)

Paxman, G. 1987. *How To Use Relaxation and Imagery with Children*. Salt Lake City: Learning Potentials. (audio)

———1987. *Imagine That!* Salt Lake City: Learning Potentials. (audio)

———1987. *Deep Relaxation*. Salt Lake City: Learning Potentials. (audio)

Rosenholtz, S. 1988. *Awareness Through Movement: The Feldenkrals Method*. San Mateo, Calif.: ABA Physical Therapy Associates. (video)

Stone, R. 1993. *Mind/Body Communication*. Niles, Ill.: Nightingale Conant Corporation. (audio)

———1991. *The Silva Method*. Niles, Ill.: Nightingale Conant Corporation. (audio)

Teaching to the Brain. 1994. Teacher TV episode 35. VHS. Washington, D. C.: National Education Association and The Learning Channel. (video)

The Mind. 1988. Vol. 1-9. New York: WNET and BBC-TV. (video)

RESOURCES:

PDP Products Catalog
  12015 North July Avenue
  Hugo, Minnesota 55038
  612-439-8865
  612-439-0421 (Fax)

Sportime Abilitations Catalog
  One Sportime Way
  Atlanta, Georgia 30340
  1-800-850-8602
  1-800-845-1535 (Fax)

Flaghouse Catalog
  150 North MacQuesten Parkway
  Mt. Vernon, New York 10550
  1-800-793-7900
  1-800-793-7922 (Fax)

Therapy Works, Inc.
   4901 Butte Place N. W.
   Albuquerque, New Mexico 87120
   505-899-4071 (Fax)

*St. John's University Center for the Study of
Learning and Teaching Styles*
   Utopia Parkway
   Jamaica, New York 11439
   718-990-6335
   718-990-6096 (Fax)